On The Road With
George Melly

On The Road With
George Melly

The final bows of a legend

Digby Fairweather

First published in Great Britain in 2007 by JR Books,
10 Greenland Street, London NW1 0ND
www.jrbooks.com

A catalogue record for this book is available from the British
Library.

ISBN 978-1-906217-32-7

1 3 5 7 9 10 8 6 4 2

Typeset by SX Composing DTP, Rayleigh, Essex
Printed by MPG Books, Bodmin, Cornwall

For:

Lisa Bridgey
My Half-Dozen
Jack Higgins
(without whom it would never have happened)

Diana Melly, his nearest,
and, of course, for

George.

Contents

	Introduction	ix
Chapter One	Meeting Mr Melly	1
Chapter Two	All Those Years Ago	11
Chapter Three	The Road to Harlech	27
Chapter Four	Getting on the Record	33
Chapter Five	Travelling Shoes and Blues	45
Chapter Six	Ronnie's and Beyond	53
Chapter Seven	Ribs, Gags and Rows	61
Chapter Eight	Blues for Watford Gap	71
Chapter Nine	On the Road and Radio	77
Chapter Ten	Back in the Groove	85
Chapter Eleven	The Madness of King George	95
Chapter Twelve	Slowing Down for Sure	111
Chapter Thirteen	Sadness in Great Ones	125
Chapter Fourteen	Farewell Old King	139

INTRODUCTION

He Knew All About It!

George Melly knew I was writing this book. 'With or without the help of Dr Smirnoff's' he twinkled – aware that mutual ingestion of our favoured drinks (mine Smirnoff's vodka, his Jameson's Irish whiskey) occasionally – though never permanently – tempered our feelings of firm mutual affection.

I loved George of course. And writing this book about his last years – which at one point I was going to title *Winding Up* – was one way of returning a cherished favour. Back in 1965, while still a junior assistant in Southend on Sea's Central Library, I read his first volume of autobiography *Owning Up* – that now-legendary account of his fourteen youthful years on the road with the uproarious, unrepentant Mick Mulligan band – and, until I turned jazz music into my profession twelve years later, the book became my behavioural *vade-mecum*; a raver's primer. *Owning Up* to *Winding Up*; well, it seemed reasonable.

In the intervening years I'd read most of his other volumes of autobiography as well. These included a comprehensive and conscientious account of his early life in Liverpool (*Scouse Mouse*) in which his gift for microscopic recall of every tiny detail of people and things around him turned the pages ablaze with local colour. Then there was *Rum, Bum and Concertina* (probably inevitably an account of his Navy days) and then of course *Owning Up*. Another one – now long out-of-print – was *Mellymobile*; a series of articles written for *Punch* magazine which (unlike George) I adored, as they seemed to me to encapsulate two of his greatest qualities; a sublime receptivity to – and celebration of – humanity.

Then, after we started to travel the jazz roads regularly together in 2003, I was aware that he was conscientiously cataloguing the trials and challenges of gathering old age (in *Slowing Down* published in 2005). It was – and remains – a humorous, brave and deeply touching account of a convinced iconoclast shouting defiance at the reaper. It seemed almost as if George would welcome the chance to write a full account of his final departure from the world; a definitive full stop, dictated from above.

But in this last vivid chronicle of the processes and indignities of ageing, many stories of an irreplaceable cultural icon and jazz singer and his collaboration with Digby Fairweather's Half-Dozen – scandalous, touching, regularly hilarious – remained untold. And inside these pages are what I remember of them over the six tumultuous years from 2002 to 2007.

Need I say that I loved his singing and that the chance to work and collaborate with him musically from 2002 was an opportunity I seized, then cherished? Hopefully not. But like many of the rest of his world, I loved George as a human being too. As people we were different, yet similar; both middle-class, with concomitant middle-class rebellions close to our surfaces. Regularly in our early days we would discover mutual enthusiasms and re-enthuse over them; Noel Coward, the diaries of George and Weedon Grossmith's *Nobody* and E.M. Delafield's *Provincial Lady*. Of course we both enjoyed writing too; an intellectual commitment, shared but seldom discussed. However, regularly I was aware of a deeper mental communion between us; seldom expressed – partially because of the barring clause that was his deafness – but which allowed me, in scattered statements, to recognise a friend and fellow thinker with whom I would have valued much more conversation time earlier on in his life.

Even so, Melly-truths – expressed as part of his on-stage, and off-stage show – regularly rang profound bells within me. An example? Well, here's just one. 'Jelly Roll Morton,' he would say, 'was the biggest liar in jazz. But sometimes lies can express a truth more clearly than the truth itself.' How true indeed. Very often too I was aware of a different sort of subliminal mental link between us. During our performing years together George and I both drank, sometimes heavily. And even amid an onstage mist I knew what he was about to do or say; when some piece of business might be inadvertently missed or other long-forgotten ad lib triumphantly restored to his presentation. It was as if we moved, in some strange way, along semi-recognised parallel mental lines of communication.

So this is the story – regularly outrageous, as was *Owning Up* – of our years together. The laughs and spats. The good music and the chaos. The gentle considerations (George was a kind man) and occasional drunken disregards. It's a small return for that 1965 primer and for an artistic and personal collaboration which I shall value until the day I, in turn, complete that 'slowing down' process and stop for good.

And who knows, perhaps thereafter? George wouldn't have liked that slipped-in phrase. He always professed certainty that once life was done that was it, although once avowing – in a semi-acknowledgement of some sort of misty (if less than sanitary) afterlife – that if anybody came to his funeral wearing black he would look down from above and shit on them from a great height. Well I suppose that's something. I remain more cautious, remembering the wistful words of P.G. Wodehouse: 'we'll just have to wait and see!'. But wherever he is, I hope that George can take delight in this book and laugh with all of us at the memories it contains.

Thank you, George.

Digby Fairweather

CHAPTER ONE

Meeting Mr Melly

It was on a sunny day in July 2002 that the telephone rang in my office.

'Jack Higgins here!'

The words sent a frisson through my head, and my stomach – as usual – tightened. Speaking, or more accurately barking, to me in his usual fighting-fit mode was Britain's most powerful and respected agent for jazz music. By now I had got to know him quite well. Since 1994 Jack had represented the Great British Jazz Band which I had co-led with Pete Strange and also the Best of British Jazz in which I had replaced Kenny Baker since 2000. Jack was equally capable of laying one hand on every top act in Britain from Humphrey Lyttelton to Jools Holland, and handing them a hearty slap with the other if they didn't come up with the goods. His reaction to day-to-day events was similarly realistic, down to earth and tough. One day, shortly after the traumas of 11 September 2001 had shaken the world, the subject came up between us during a telephone conversation.

'It's terrible, isn't it?' I offered.

'What's all the fuss about?' roared my full-time colleague-to-be. 'Bloody Americans! We had all that all the way through

1

the Blitz and we're still here. What's the matter with the weak-kneed bastards?' It was impossible not to like this straight-talking tough guy.

Jack evinced mingled respect and apprehension in all his clients. His temper if roused (which it easily could be) was legendarily fearsome. And his verbal contracts with clients – never issued in print, or signed – were based on a lifelong verbal ability to bully any subversive into meek submission.

'Jack! Good morning! What can I do for you?' I said.

'Now, my friend. How would you feel about working with George Melly? The Feetwarmers are disbanding at Christmas and he needs a band.'

The Feetwarmers putting their feet up after thirty years? This was news indeed and I caught my breath. 'Well, of course . . .'

Jack cut in. 'You may be required for a concert in Harlech. Establish the band's availability next month – Sunday, 25 August – and let me know. Immediately.' The phone went dead.

Unbelievable news indeed, but good for me. Despite good reviews, stable talented personnel and even a successful album *Twelve Feet Off The Ground* for the Carlisle-based Flat Five Records back in 1998, my band, Digby Fairweather's Half-Dozen, had been struggling for eight years now to establish itself in small clubs and cut-price gigs at London venues. We had formed first in 1994, fulfilling a new ambition for me – to work with younger players, play a far wider variety of material than I had been tackling hitherto and, most particularly, to have a vocal group within the band. I adored classic vocal ensembles from the Four Freshmen back to Six Hits and a Miss and beyond and deeply wanted to re-examine the genre. So new colleagues and confrères were necessary. First I'd approached the multi-talented Julian Marc Stringle, who not only played glorious clarinet and saxophones but also had – I was soon to discover – a voice of choirboy quality. He also looked like a young Marc Bolan, ran the London Marathon for several years and covered seven more miles a day just to keep in trim. With a young and gifted trombonist-singer Malcolm Earle Smith and brilliant emergent pianist Craig Milverton, we had debuted our close harmony vocals at the Clacton Jazz Festival 1997, after a round-the-piano rehearsal in the auditorium of the Prince's Theatre. Our repeated rendition of the touching ballad 'Time Was' had evinced our first public critique from its longtime stage manager George, on duty early one morning and already full of his favoured brew, Pusser's Rum.

'Oh no!' said George after our sixth try. 'Not that bleedin' thing again!'

But luckily, in the sun-soaked afternoon where we sang on open-mike to a lazy, happy crowd basking in deck chairs, the reaction was more positive and we knew that something musically good was taking shape.

It was a year later – at Clacton again, and thanks to Julian's ever-generous introduction – that we were joined by a young and sensational guitarist, Dominic Ashworth. And by 2002 – after Malcolm had left to join rock star Brian Ferry and Julian had taken over the lead-vocal chores – our band had permanently stabilised to include, besides Julian, a fine and under-valued jazz trombonist Chris Gower (whose CV included work with Shakin' Stevens, Suzi Quatro, Graham Parker, Jess Roden and Sir Cliff Richard as well as numerous premier-league big bands), Craig, Dominic, legendary bassist Len Skeat and drummer Bobby Worth (both highly experienced and deeply skilled jazz-based sessionmen). We were rehearsed to the nines and had an act that was crying out for wider exposure.

Joining George Melly – one of Britain's most celebrated humanists, singers, art connoisseurs, authors and all-round cultural icons – would, I knew, be a huge step up in terms of exposure and prestige. And, I couldn't help thinking too, it would open stylistic doors and avenues for George that had been impracticable within the small traditional quartet format of John Chilton's Feetwarmers. After all, I reasoned, we carried an all-electric rhythm section, a vocal group of four singers, and three horns. My mind was already flying ahead.

But then a thought occurred to me. What about John Chilton? What had really happened? Was this legendary partnership of thirty years really coming to an end at last? I rang John to make sure.

'Yes,' he said, 'I know all about this. And I think it's true. You don't have to worry, Dig. Go ahead!' And in the post, a day or so later, came a comprehensive typed list of George's current repertoire complete with keys. Kind yet methodical, John was, as ever, true to his word.

Then one August Wednesday soon after, in a café just outside Manchester Piccadilly station, my mobile phone rang. 'Higgins here!' roared the voice. 'Don't fuck about! I'm busy! Get a pen and paper.'

'Hang on just one second, Jack,' I said.

'What?' I had seldom heard more angry volume poured into a single word.

'I'm in a greasy spoon,' I stammered, 'in Manchester. And some of the grease is on the paper.' Which it was. But by leaning my full weight on a discarded daily, and willing my biro not to give in, I was ready to take down the barked instructions that followed.

'Right! You'll need to meet George as soon as possible. Here's a list of numbers. Take them down. George's first – though he seldom answers. If you want to make any plans, you'll probably need to speak to Diana, his wife. Here's her London number and her country number; they've got a second place in Bagnor. No, not Bangor! Bagnor – near Reading.

There's a fax number; here it is. George can see you all day this Friday, Saturday or Sunday. And after that 20 to 22 of August. Have you got that? Well, get to it.' Click.

A day later a charming, twittering voice came on the phone. 'Hello, Digby! This is George's secretary here, Shirley. And he'd like to meet you. When would be convenient?'

'Well,' I said, scanning my diary, 'how about Saturday, 17 August? Jack Higgins told me he was free that day. Around midday perhaps?'

'That sounds fine,' said the obliging Shirley. 'And George is here and he'd like to speak to you.'

A rich plummy voice came on the phone. 'Hi, Digby – George here!'

'How nice to hear you,' I said, meaning it.

'Come along on Saturday,' said my hospitable host-to-be, 'and I'll buy you lunch!'

'That sounds lovely,' I said. 'But you must be secretly feeling that all of this is a damn nuisance.'

'Why?'

'Well, having to start all over again with a new band after thirty years . . .'

'Not at all,' said George Melly. 'I'll tell you all about it when I see you. Bye bye, dear.'

Saturday, 17 August was the hottest day of 2002. So in a white-shirted defence against the heat and loose slacks I set off to meet my hero. But, careless of Shirley's carefully expressed instructions, I arrived at the wrong station (there are two christened Shepherd's Bush) and armed only with an expensive bottle of Chivas Regal, wandered east along Holland Park Avenue to find myself staring bemusedly at Royal Crescent where, I remembered, the great 'Who will buy' scene from *Oliver* had been filmed. But this was no time for movie trivia; plainly I was well off course. Into a taxi then, and back we drove around Shepherd's Bush Green, before finally arriving at a narrow neat street in which modern flats mixed a shade uneasily with terraced Victorian houses. A bright red gate greeted me – possibly George was publicly airing his left-wing convictions – and beyond it an equally brightly painted front door pinned with a notice demanding the swift departure of hawkers, circulars, fish-sellers, knife sharpeners, Tories, sexist men and related undesirables. I rang the bell but there was no answer.

Perhaps he's out, I thought and rang it again several times to an equally persistent non-response. So at last I salvaged my mobile phone from my shoulder bag, rang the newly acquired number and the same rich voice answered the call.

'Digby! Is that you? Where are you?'

'Outside,' I said, 'Have I come at a bad moment?'

'Not at all! Exactly the right time. I'll come and let you in.'

Clad in royal-blue tank-bottoms, a T-shirt and resplendent purple waistcoat, my host made his steady way to the door and opened it. 'So good to see you, Sir George,' I said.

'And you too. Come upstairs.'

Through a hall fringed with waist-high cupboards we went up some dim brown stairs, past a hatstand blossoming with ornate and colourful headgear; then up again to a lounge in which the sun glanced through the window on to a table equipped with computer, printer and office accessories. Next to it stood an antique desk with notebooks neatly arranged amid paperweights, ornaments and a penholder. I handed my host the Chivas Regal.

'Oh! That's a nice present,' he said. 'It's my birthday tomorrow, you know. Seventy-six.'

I had had no idea. But as he unwrapped the whiskey I glanced briefly around his living-room; its walls decorated with abstract art in several dimensions, a circular table well stocked with bottles and glasses, a long bookshelf full of volumes of art at floor level and a deep brown leather armchair on which a now-famous parody of George's familiar face had been embroidered in loving cartoon detail. George noticed my gaze.

'I had a chiropodist in the other day,' he observed, 'and I asked her if she wanted to sit on my face. She was not amused.'

'So,' I said, 'tell me about what's been happening.'

'Well,' said George, 'it had stopped being so much fun with the Feetwarmers; we'd all been getting rather bored. And Harlech this year was a benchmark. John had been getting very tired and our agent Jack Higgins had had a job cancelled just before a one-nighter there. John said, "We don't want to go all the way over there for a one-nighter! I'm not going, George. And I want you to back me up." So, I said, "OK." But when Higgins phoned me and I said "no" he said, "Well, in that case I won't get you any work at all next year – or ever again." So I caved in but John would not. And I think he expected that the Feetwarmers would do it with a deputy trumpeter, which they've done before when John was ill. But this time that didn't happen. John was getting very frustrated with all the travelling and routine anyhow. And lately he's become so stressed. If something goes wrong, it's like "fuck, fuck, fuck!".' George's eyes were innocently wide. 'And I said, "John, please don't keep saying that. It upsets me seeing you like this." But it didn't do any good.'

There had been other troubles with the Feetwarmers too. A cancelled Christmas bonus due to lack of funds after their last Christmas season at Ronnie Scott's had provoked a bad row with one member. And one in particular had incurred George's increasing wrath. 'Him! I can't stand him! One day he came to the breakfast table and said, "Can I join you?" And I SCREAMED at him [George, I was soon to find out, often talked in capital letters], "No! You can't. You are annoying, stupid and tedious and I want nothing to do with you. Go and sit somewhere else.'" Plainly the Feetwarmers had not always considered the social clause in their employment policies.

Later we walked, in bright sunlight, from the house towards Shepherd's Bush Green. George was sporting a bright-pink knitted shoulder bag. 'I wear one too,' I observed.

'Not so poofy as mine,' returned my companion.

On the way we stopped at a service laundry run by a pretty Indonesian girl, and George emptied a large carrier bag of laundry on to her counter. 'Yours, my dear!' he said. 'Oh look at that lovely Rastafarian art on the wall of the railway bridge. You didn't notice that, did you? I thought not! Let's go and look.'

We stopped to admire the graffiti before making our way to a Shepherd's Bush brasserie where my host received a big welcome from the owner. 'We'll drink gazpacho,' George said. 'You don't know what that is, do you?' I had to admit that I didn't.

'It's cold soup,' said George when it arrived, 'delicious!' And emptied the bowl by lifting it to his lips. 'I've got a couple of broadcasts later on this afternoon,' he continued, 'then lecturing later at the Tate – Matisse and Picasso. It's not until 11 p.m.; part of an all-nighter. It finishes at 7 a.m.'

'That's late,' I said, 'but you look fit and fine!'

'In general, yes,' said George, 'but in a month or so I have to have that thing with the tube down my throat. Monday, 19 September. Yes, that's it; an endoscopy. Something amiss in my stomach apparently but I've no idea what. About twenty years ago I had an expensive set of tests for stomach ulcers: blow down a tube – squeeze-blow and so on. But the first two times nothing worked and it was expensive. So I said, "I'm not here to be a bankrupt guinea pig."'

The talk turned to our first date at Harlech the following week, and I mentioned a couple of tunes and programme order.

George readily agreed; apparently he was the most easy-going and co-operative of musical partners. 'Now,' he said with a wicked grin, 'after this you can tell Jack we spent the WHOLE lunchtime working out a programme.'

After a pause, he called the maître-d'hôtel to the table. 'Does anyone smoke here?' he asked.

'No one on the staff, sir. I'm sorry.'

'There's a pretty blonde over there who's smoking,' I said. 'See her – talking to her boyfriend?'

'Oh yes.' George strolled across and returned a minute or two later with his free cigarette.

'Did she know you?' I asked.

'Don't think so,' said George. 'If she did, she didn't let on. Well, now, you're going to the station.'

I wasn't sure if this was an observation or a gentle command but together in the afternoon sun we walked back towards the tube. 'Where's Diana today?' I asked.

'In the country,' said George. 'We have a loose relationship. If she's in the country I'm generally in town, and vice versa. Lovely little arse!' he added unexpectedly.

I looked over and a pretty young girl had passed us. It was obvious that the Dean of Decadence was far from his retirement date yet. We shook hands at the tube station and I watched my wonderful new friend make his stately way back towards home in the Shepherd's Bush sunlight as I remembered how my musico-cultural love affair with him had begun all of 41 years before.

CHAPTER TWO

All Those Years Ago

It was the rough-edged but enchantingly lyrical voice providing a seductive three-minute jazz interlude on 'Saturday Club', sometime in 1961, that had persuaded me that I'd discovered for myself a jazz singer who was special. The song was 'Sweet Lorraine' and the young singer was – of course – my musical partner-to-be, George Melly.

At that point, of course, I had no idea of this and I didn't know that much about George Melly either. He sang with a famous band led by trumpeter Mick Mulligan, and they toured Britain, made records, of course, and appeared on radio as well as television. We'd just acquired a television, after years of determined resistance by my father (who preferred his beloved gramophone and regularly growing collection of classical LPs), and one night I tuned in on a short show, in grainy black and white, featuring my newly discovered band and singer. An informal thing, in which the voice-over announcer talked about the 'grainy trumpet of Mick Mulligan' and George committed to television history his spectacular version of 'Frankie and Johnny', turning his back to the camera to simulate, with his own hands stroking his back, a couple in passionate embrace. It was a striking idea, which David Bowie would (consciously or not) also use years later (no doubt with George's approval) for his 'Heroes' video.

But for now that was just about it. I sensed vaguely that Mulligan and Melly had a 'reputation'; big enough for one LP – on which they were paired with the 'Saints' jazz band from Manchester – to be titled *The Saints Meet the Sinners*. Beyond that, though, there was nothing much to go on.

That is (or was) until 1965 when – as a smiling young trainee librarian in Southend Central Library – I discovered George's first autobiography *Owning Up*, and snatched it away from the 'New titles' section. Reading – or rather devouring – it in our nearby coffee bar, in fits of laughter, a whole new world opened up; a world of all-night jazz, wild drinking, damp digs and lumbering back a scrubber to the room, if you hadn't already had a knee-tremble with her behind the club halfway through the job.

Virtuously, George had shown the text of his proposed books to all the friends and partners whose eccentricities – and on-the-road excesses – might have given cause for offence, domestic problems or even a libel suit. All had agreed bar one: trombonist Frank Parr who, before his alliance with Mick Mulligan's band, had shown huge promise as a potential member of Lancashire's cricket team. Among much other intimate detail, Frank's portrait included a detailed description of his regular inspection of his own armpits for spectacular body odour, self-described with pride as 'going a bit'. But none of this bothered him at all. What did was George's description of him as 'wicket-keeper'. 'Damn it,' said Parr in a fury, 'everyone knows the phrase is "kept wicket".' All else was well. And, as my good friend cornettist Alex Welsh laughingly pointed out in later years, it was only George's own excesses that were the occasional victims of self-censorship.

For a middle-class boy, raised in the sedate but hungover

post-war years of victorious Britain – publicly entertained by the *Billy Cotton Band Show, Dixon of Dock Green* and the received-English of the BBC – this book was, to say the very least, an eye-opener. Vilified by the then poet laureate Philip Larkin (who, as a university librarian with a clutch of well-separated girlfriends, was in no real position to preach moral virtue), it achieved widespread notoriety and changed my life for at least a couple of decades. Admittedly the Beatles had, by then, cleared away all the stale air of Tin Pan Alley and the sixties were here. But *Owning Up* made it very plain that people had been swinging long before the sixties; as Bill Le Sage, the great British musician, told me in 1991, while I was trumpet tutor at Sir John Dankworth's Wavendon summer school, 'We taught the Rolling Stones all they knew.' And that wasn't just music! Growing up through the Southend music scene, trumpet with me at every available second, I decided – to the regular confusion of my steadier friends – that outrageousness was the way forward. Proper knee-trembles were out of the question. The Pill hadn't arrived and I was far too shy to buy condoms, or 'rubber johnnies' as we called them then. But, by 1973 (in the appropriately anarchic atmosphere of Dave Claridge's marvellous New Orleans Jazz Band), I certainly wasn't above a good feel-up with a friendly local girl in the band car park and a nightly vocal rerendition of 'Nuts' in tribute to my hero.

'Nuts' was important. It was the naughty rewrite of the old jazz tune 'Jada', made famous by blues singer Roosevelt 'The Honeydripper' Sykes, that had brought George Melly directly back in the spotlight. And thanks to *Owning Up*, I knew a lot more about him. After the Beatles had created the twentieth century's most dramatic redefinition of popular culture, he had more or less abandoned singing to become a TV critic and prolific journalist, often to be seen, read and heard. 'Mr Melly, the man on the Telly' indeed. A later book, *Revolt into Style*, proved that this remarkable man – unlike many of his more sullen jazz contemporaries – was, like myself, well open to the rock-revolution music that formed the yang to my own jazz yin. But it was in the pages of the *Melody Maker* – frequently at the championship of their marvellous critic Chris Welch – that George appeared most clearly to be refocusing attention on his singing, appearing, by the late 1960s, as a solo attraction with bands around London and perfectly fitting the times with his outrageousness. And, of course, his bisexuality. This was the era of David Bowie and the idea (as well as everything else, so it seemed) was definitely in.

And then, thanks to the Beatles' publicist, Derek Taylor, plus Welch and burgeoning publicity during the rock years, George had had his hit album *Nuts*. It was produced in 1972 by his great friend Taylor and you couldn't miss it on the shelves. With a slot-in portrait of the man framed within its front cover and captioned 'Wouldn't this photograph make a good enlargement' the album was no nostalgic retro, but an unashamed product of its time, complete with tributes from six contemporaries, including Max Jones, Michael Kustow and Mick Mulligan. Mick's encomium reassured us that the tales of *Owning Up* had been truer than true. 'You could never find a better mate than George, be it man, woman or bulldog,' Mick wrote (later on I would get to the bottom of this bizarre triumvirate). 'During some dozen years of weekly forays into the jungles of the scrubber belt, our George entertained, amused and generally knocked out not only the audiences but also ourselves as well. One of the Great Architect's better efforts!'

But my favourite tribute came from Annie Ross. Annie – my vocalese heroine – whose voice had led the great group Lambert Hendricks and Ross; who had sung with Lionel

Hampton, Clifford Brown and Dizzy Gillespie; who was an icon of the modern jazz movement. And whose final top note in 'Down for the Count' in the *Sing a Song of Basie* album had kept me awake for three whole nights one school weekend when I was fourteen. Wow! If she liked George then he simply had to be the greatest thing. Annie's tribute was a poem which cleverly summarised almost all of George's obsessions – from hats to blues – and included the humorous and affectionate lines:

> He loves to eat
> And he digs Magritte
> . . . George Melly I love you!'

The *Nuts* album was George's recorded gateway to a new career as jazz singer with John Chilton's Feetwarmers and the progress of a jazz singer into the charts dominated, or indeed ruled, by rock music was a source of fascination to me. However, still I was enthralled by *Owning Up* and those raver's years on the road with Mick Mulligan.

But it was in the later 1960s that I first saw George sing: at a concert at Camden's Roundhouse in the good company of Alex Welsh's great band and French tenorist Guy Lafitte, accompanied by Keith Ingham's Trio. Unaccountably, one corner of the stage was occupied by a swarthy bearded tramp peacefully dozing through the proceedings. Far from fazed, my hero greeted the insurgent with a friendly wave, jovial greeting and clap on the shoulder for good measure as he passed him to sing. There's a man, I thought, who likes life and people and takes everything in good spirit.

Years later I would get to know not only George but Mick Mulligan too. Sometimes on my visits to the south coast with Val Wiseman's *Lady Sings the Blues* show, he would turn up with an aristocratic south coast trumpet triumvirate completed by Kenny Baker and Nat Gonella, and lent his experienced ear to what was happening on the stage. With jutting eyebrows (somewhat ressembling devil's horns), firmly placed handsome features, piercing blue eyes, public-school delivery and a charm that made his every statement sound like a declaration of affection, outrageous or not, it was easy to see why his singer of fourteen years, George Melly, loved him for life. And so I was delighted when, in 1984, as a contributor to the definitive and prestigious *Grove's Dictionary of Jazz*, I was asked to write an entry on Mick Mulligan. I rang his number.

'Mick Mulligan here.'

'Mr Mulligan,' I said, 'I've been asked to include you in *Grove's Dictionary*. And I'd very much like to know whether you mind – and, if not, if I might ask a few questions?'

'Go ahead, cock.' To Mick most people, apart from lady friends, were 'cock'.

'Well,' I said, 'I'm afraid one of the things I need is your date of birth.'

'Twenty-fourth of January, 1928,' said my interviewee. 'So that day I'll have a drink with you.'

'Certainly,' I said, 'and, by the way, that's my girlfriend's birthday too.'

'Good,' returned Mr Mulligan. 'So I'll have a drink with you – and a fuck with her!'

During the interview that followed I asked Mick when he had formed the Magnolia Jazz Band. '1948,' was the reply. 'So when did you take up the trumpet?' '1948.' Remarkable!

As the years went by I found out a lot more about Mick. Devastatingly charming, very well spoken (a BBC dramatisation of the Mulligan years once miscast him as a cockney) and incapable of offence even at his most outrageous; he had lived, for a time in the fifties, during his bandleading days, in Lisle

Street, Soho – a haven for prostitutes. One hot day Mick had been sitting on the steps outside his house chatting to the girls.

'Oh, love!' said one. 'It's so hot. And you know what that does to men. I must have been up and down those stairs fourteen times already.'

'Oh, darling,' said Mick Mulligan, 'your poor *feet!*'

Mick adored women – and they fell for him too – but he could be impatient with inappropriate company. After one exhausting session with George and his band at 100 Oxford Street, he found himself surrounded by female admirers and one chosen friend who persistently interrupted his conversation. Mick finally turned to her in exasperation.

'Darling,' he said disparagingly. 'Just shut up, will you. Or the fuck's off!'

Mick could handle himself well too as George knew from his efficient dispatch of a teddy boy one evening from the well-remembered Cooks Ferry Inn – a legendary home of British Dixieland jazz in the 1950s. On another occasion he had watched a female friend in the crowds being over-familiarly tackled by a bystander; so he walked over and told him in no uncertain terms to leave her alone. Mick returned to his friend looking satisfied.

'There,' he said. 'Now that must be worth a handful of tit, mustn't it?'

Mick had given up bandleading in the early 1960s and retired to run an off licence. And of course after ten more years George had returned to the road with John Chilton's Feetwarmers to a second starry career. Much later, during the 1990s, by which time they had completed over twenty of their thirty years on the road, I had been corralled from an eighteen-month sojourn on Jazz FM into the service of the BBC. Initially as a substitute for my close friend and champion the late Peter Clayton, known to most as 'the voice of jazz' in Britain, I spent a less-than-secure five years on a variety of shows including the World Service's *Jazz for the Asking*, *Jazz Parade* and later *Jazz Notes*. These last two were half-hour shows – first five a week, later four – that were notable for their transmission in or after the midnight hour when all but the most devoted jazz fans or lonely women were dozing off in their thousands.

One welcome interviewee was George and I'd decided that it would be a good idea to reunite my guest with his old bandleader. So, under the bemused gaze of my producer Terry Carter, I dialled Mick on a BBC line-out while George sat opposite me in the studio.

'Hello, Mick,' I said brightly. 'George is here and waiting. And I thought it might be fun if I introduced him and then said, "Mick Mulligan, welcome back to the airwaves. And I've got a young singer here who's looking for a job and wondered if he might have a word with you." There was a compliant grunt from the other end of the phone and Terry Carter rolled the tapes.

'Good evening,' I said, 'welcome to tonight's *Jazz Notes*. Tonight our guests are legendary trumpeter Mick Mulligan and a newcomer to the scene – a singer who's looking for work. Mick, would you mind having a word?'

'Hello, you old cunt!' responded the obliging Mick. 'How's things?'

Bells rang, lights flashed and the rage infusing my prurient producer's face indicated that we had a problem. Luckily we weren't live and therefore in need of the seven-second delay mechanism universally known to live radio broadcasters as the 'fuck-button'.

'Mr Mulligan,' said Carter, scarlet-faced, 'we'll have no more of that kind of language on my show. If you please!'

But it was very difficult to stem Mick's regular return to basic Anglo-Saxon and, rather than 'de-um' him later ('de-umming' is the editing process of eliminating unfortunate false starts and stops after an interview is recorded), we couldn't even de-eff Mick and – to my great regret – the whole idea and interview were scrapped.

But this was in the 1990s. Meanwhile, back in the early 1970s, I was still a full-time librarian with trumpet attached and just starting to make my way up the jazz ladder into professional company. Among a slew of other ambitions I knew that somehow I had to meet George Melly, the liberator of my introverted post-pubescent years.

The chance came in about 1973 when I'd joined a professional-level traditional band, Jazz Legend, co-led by Hugh Rainey (a former star with Bob Wallis's hit-making Storyville Jazzmen) and soprano saxophonist Eggy Ley, a well-known and gifted British player, who'd made a big name for himself in Europe during Britain's trad-boom years. Every so often we played at a club in Romford called the Reservation and Eggy, who had friends all over the British jazz scene, sometimes invited guests to star with our band. An early one was a well-known British guitarist, Diz Disley, who played wonderfully (later he partnered Stephane Grappelli in Britain and beyond playing Django Reinhardt style and achieving widespread success on radio, TV and records). Diz scatted along happily with his own solos as he played: da-da-da-de-deedle-dum-da-da. Then as a string broke: da-da-de-deedle-fuck it!-da-da-deedle!

But another early guest was to be – guess who – George Melly! I was thrilled.

By now I knew that George was bisexual. Beyond the confessions of *Owning Up* I had been lucky enough to become friends with the great Dixieland bandleader Alex Welsh, who always announced one of his favourite tunes as '"She's Funny That Way", a tune we dedicate to George Melly'. I was intrigued but wary; at that time I was both slim and sported more long blonde hair than Roger Daltrey. And Pete Thornett, a wonderful East End gentleman who played bass with Jazz Legend, was wickedly ecstatic. 'You be careful, Dig,' he warned. 'He'll be up your bum before you know it.'

Young still, beautifully dressed and full of star presence, George arrived and in due course joined the band on-stage. In a passionate version of 'Backwater Blues' I took a long down-home trumpet solo, eyes closed, and towards the end heard a delighted bellow from the bass department: 'Told you!'

As I opened my eyes I found my hero close at my side; bedroom-eyes focused firmly in my direction. Unabashed, at half-time nonetheless, I lined up with a bevy of fellow fans to have my well-thumbed copy of *Owning Up* autographed by my hero. And in doing so used a term to George inherited from my library days to try to explain how the book had altered my way of seeing life.

'It was bibliotherapeutic,' I explained helpfully.

'What?' said George, mystified. Possibly he was already suffering from the deafness that would assail him in later years, but the word itself was no doubt enough to stop the conversation. So that was that.

The next time I saw him around was in the early 1980s at New Merlin's Cave, the legendary home for the mainstream fraternity which flourished every Sunday lunchtime in Clerkenwell. As well as the dirtiest lavatory facilities in London, the Cave had a crèche for children, and played host to the cream of London's players in that style. Visit Merlin's on Sunday and you could hear (regularly) John Chilton, Bruce Turner and Wally Fawkes, as well as such eminent sitters-in as Kathy Stobart, trumpeter Colin Smith, pianist Collin Bates, and American visitors such as Al Grey and Jonah Jones, who would come in search of a blow. And usually at side-stage, immaculately dressed in pinstripe suit and fedora hat, would be George Melly, digging the sounds and waiting to sing.

Another Merlin's fixture was Sally. She was beautiful; a generously proportioned, curvaceous dream of a woman with formidable breasts, which she joyfully shook in time to the music. She had been a long-time lover of a well-known jazz broadcaster and writer. But, at least once she strayed – with George.

'I took her home,' George told me later, 'and when we got into the bedroom I noticed that all around she had pictures of herself. A narcissist you see. So I suggested that if I fucked her from behind she could look at the pictures while she was doing it. Which pleased her very much and after we'd come she said, "You're the only man who's ever realised that about me." But unfortunately afterwards I needed to piss and Sally said, "It's the door down the corridor on the left." So I went down, still naked and half-erect, and opened the wrong door! And there was a full dinner party going on, which rather surprised them.'

By the early 1970s George's career with the Feetwarmers – now reduced to the quartet of John Chilton, Collin Bates, Steve Fagg and drummer Chuck Smith (known to the fraternity for the generous volume of his performance as 'Hammer' Smith) – was beginning to show signs of taking off in a big way. Having found themselves in the album charts (a near-impossible situation for a British jazz group at that time), John and George had agreed to management by the Ronnie Scott organisation, in the personage of 'Chips' Chipperfield, a well-known man-about-jazz whose collections would later form the founding collection of Britain's National Jazz Archive. As a manager, however, Chips was inexperienced and had no idea how to deal with such a big-time situation in the making. A trip to the USA to explore tours for the group had produced muted responses from young rock-based producers at Warner Brothers.

Finally, in January 1974, George and John invaded Ronnie Scott's to ask what – if anything – was going on. And there they were confronted by Jack Higgins. Jack had cut his teeth running small clubs in west London during the late 1940s and rapidly moved on to bigger things; first in the West End and later with the great Harold Davison agency. With Davison he had taken charge of the jazz side of activities, bringing to England top American jazz acts, including the Modern Jazz Quartet, Gerry Mulligan, Louis Armstrong, Duke Ellington and Count Basie, and pop groups, such as the Supremes. During these years he had learned to deal hard with every one of his clients. Since the mid-1960s he had concentrated on traditional jazz and swing, bringing in Americans, from Buck Clayton to an alcoholic Dickie Wells, and championing the causes of British artists, from Humphrey Lyttelton to Alex Welsh.

In short, Jack was already the most highly regarded agent in Britain and George and John explained their quandary to him. 'Come back tomorrow,' said Higgins 'at 10 a.m.' Chips Chipperfield was corralled into a permanent position at the telephone calling venues up and down Britain – everything from pubs and clubs upwards – all of whom confirmed that, yes, they wanted George Melly and the Feetwarmers. At ten the next morning, Melly and Chilton arrived back in the office, and Higgins handed them a full datesheet for three months. From January 1974 the bill-topping act of George Melly and John Chilton's Feetwarmers was on its way.

And soon after Jack would join them, leaving the Scott offices to set up independent management and steer the fortunes of his new hit-making clients.

For the next thirty years they remained at the top of the tree. There were tours of China and (earlier on) a triumphant trip to New York in 1978 to play at the famous jazz venue Michael's

Pub. It was here that George was famously attacked in *The New York Post* by a prominent American critic who condemned him as a 'squat, leering figure of androgynous sexuality' as well as a 'stylistically frivolous performer of camp vaudeville'. This demoralising dismissal was swiftly countered in *The New York Times* by a second commentator, the near-legendary John S. Wilson, who praised his subject as 'An Englishman who sings like Bessie Smith' in a full half-page review which George later described as 'the kind an artist might dream of in his bath but never receive'.

Apart from two reviews in the British press by one critic notorious for both suspect guitar-playing and a declared championship of jazz's 'cutting edge', George seldom received bad reviews or even poor public commentary from musical associates. One notable exception was a New York-based musician who made no secret of his hearty dislike for 'Britain's Bessie Smith'.

'I know exactly why!' George confided to me later with a wicked twinkle. 'One night going home in the cab very drunk, I gave him a wank! And after the pleasure had subsided he apparently, and unaccountably for me, decided to resent the fact!'

Amid such carousing days and nights, and for many years hence, George Melly and John Chilton's Feetwarmers continued their triumphant progress. There were strings of albums, a rich round of British dates and, of course, radio and television.

In his book *Mellymobile*, George, as charmingly as ever, described his year-long activities on the road in between retiring to Wales to fish in his beloved private stretch of the Usk. Theirs was a saga of success unequalled by any British jazz act in the post-rock years and would turn George into a multi-faceted cultural icon, society figure, respected art connoisseur, critic and bon vivant. As a lothario and champion of the free-love days of the sixties, so miserably turned away by Aids, George determinedly and actively railed against *Dynasty* soap operas and the post-Thatcher dumbing down of our society to politically correct posturing.

Over the years I saw George occasionally but seldom to speak to. One night at the Pizza Express in Soho in 1979 he arrived at the club to listen to the Pizza Express All Stars with whom I played at the time, with a beautiful boy on each arm. I also watched him and his act regularly. A perfect presentation, decorated by the fiery trumpet of John Chilton and his neatly assembled rhythm sections. For George, John was the perfect bandleader. Methodical, to the point where a number was never repeated on a return visit to any venue, he was also an immaculately suited but discreet backdrop to his florid frontman, backing him with a huge selection of mutes (known irreverently to fellow trumpeter John Lawrence as the 'Chilton Hundreds'), ever supporting, never competing. He was also, by report, a bandleader who set himself apart from his sidemen in traditional style. According to a gleeful George, pianist Stan Greig had retired from the band after three years complaining of the disciplinarian tendencies of 'yon martinet'. John could exert a tight rein on his wayward frontman too, pointing out if a joke went on for too long or other aspects of the show veered off course.

In future years I would fully comprehend some of these problems. And also become very fond of John himself. He is one of jazz music's most conscientious and gifted biographers, whose subjects included Sidney Bechet, Coleman Hawkins, Billie Holiday and Bob Crosby, as well as a definitive *Who's Who of British Jazz*, and his contributions to jazz bibliography were regularly celebrated by high-profile awards. His Christmas cards and occasional notes addressed to me – constantly complimentary about my contributions to the foundation and development of the National Jazz Archive and related activities – revealed a man as kind and devoted to the cause of jazz itself as he could, by all accounts, be strict about what went on on his stand. His later and very welcome autobiography *Hot Jazz Warm Feet* was also (despite George Melly's initial reservations) an honest, considered and fascinating account of a life devoted to the music, devoid of the self-preoccupation which remains an integral part of most autobiography.

So it was unquestionably due very largely to John's gifts as trumpeter, bandleader, everyday organiser and songwriter (he wrote George's perennial signature song 'Good Time George') that the Feetwarmers presented a finely honed and, in its early days, wild show. An uproarious edition of 'The Ovaltinies' (retitled 'The In-betweenies' in view of the ensemble's middle-aged status) could easily be capped on its craziest nights with the outrageous blues 'Shave 'em Dry'.

> I got nipples on my titties
> that are bigger than my thumbs!
> There's something in between my legs
> Would make a dead man come!

Only in its much later days did the show begin to display signs of polish that threatened to change to veneer. Slowly, slowly, work began to diminish. And, at the last of their thirty years' residency for the Christmas season at Ronnie Scott's (on one night of which George appeared in full drag as his own grandmother), there was the dismal row over the expected Christmas bonus, as neither George nor John was able to subsidise their sidemen. Work for George Melly and the Feetwarmers, so it was rumoured, was beginning to ease off.

Meantime, as the years rolled on, I had met all three of the principals in George's career. John Chilton, who was bespectacled, always sharply suited, kind, and committed for a lifetime to the dual causes of trumpet and jazz documentation had been the organising director for George. A striking contrast to two wonderful reprobates: one who was his bandleading forerunner, Mick Mulligan; the other his star. And now, it seemed the new bandleader was to be me.

CHAPTER THREE

The Road to Harlech

By mid-August 2002, things were starting to move ahead and fast. The two bands with whom I was already working for Jack Higgins – the Great British Jazz Band and the Best of British Jazz, which just over a month previously had finished a recording session at Abbey Road – were, like George Melly and the Feetwarmers, showing signs of losing speed. Now, with a new musical partner whose music I admired, I felt that things were certainly not what they used to be. And our first gig was only ten days ahead.

At 11.30 a.m. on 20 August the phone rang.

'Is that Lord Fairweather of Southsea?'

'Exactly so. How is your endo, now it's been scoped?'

'Eh?'

'I mean,' I said hastily, 'how was the endoscopy?'

'Fine,' said George blithely. 'They have a little thing like the thing you throw a drowning sailor. They freeze it first and it tastes filthy but once it's past the back of your throat – the cough point – you don't feel a thing. They had a good look around but found nothing, apart from a tiny patch of inflammation and two bay leaves from a curry.'

'Oh, that's good,' I said. 'And how are you travelling to Harlech?'

'I'm going over beforehand,' said George. 'And you?'

'Playing the night before,' I said, 'so I'll be driving over with Lisa, my partner, on the Sunday.'

'Then let's have a rehearsal – around 5 p.m. I shall see you there,' said George with a wicked chuckle, 'with your horn in your hand.'

Later I called Jack Higgins. 'Make it four, not five!' he commanded. 'And make sure George does enough. Sort out the lighting plan with the theatre. They're quite liable to fuck it up, you know. That's why I take my own manager and lighting person wherever I go.'

Soon after, John Chilton rang. 'I thought you might need help with a couple of keys,' he said kindly. 'And by the way don't be afraid to shout at George. He's very deaf.'

'I've heard about the "deafies",' I chuckled.

'Oh yes,' said John. 'The best one I know was when we played Uxbridge with the Feetwarmers and a lady came up and said, "I was in Uxbridge for four years." And George said, "Oh! My deepest sympathy!" The lady looked surprised and said, "No, I enjoyed it." And George said, "No, no! I really can't accept that! It must have been truly terrible." And finally the lady looked at him and said, "What did you think I said?" And George said, "You did say Auschwitz, didn't you?"'

So with the Half-Dozen booked – Julian Marc Stringle (reeds), Chris Gower (trombone), Craig Milverton (piano), Dominic Ashworth (guitar), Len Skeat (bass) and Bobby Worth (drums) – we made the long drive to Harlech. This was the gig that had finished the Feetwarmers and I could see why. It was a long way! Through often-ravishing countryside, past Snowdonia and alongside slate mines via a mass of B roads, we arrived at last after hours on the road and pulled up in the car park of Byrdyr House Hotel in the High Street.

There was George, sitting at an outside table, dressed in a multicoloured T-shirt, jogging bottoms and flip-flops peering earnestly at a copy of the *Independent*. As I approached he looked up with his usual greeting. 'Hello.'

'Hello, George,' I said, 'this is Lisa.'

'What lovely eyes,' said George, giving her an unmistakeable ooh-la-la!

'I'll be driving you to the theatre later, George,' said Lisa. 'But I'm really sorry. The car's a bit of a tip.'

'Never mind, dear,' said George. 'Just come to the bed-room – and lie down. Then we can drive to the rehearsal. I'm used to cars that look like a skip.'

And so, after a short siesta, to the theatre we went, to run through our show. I had sketched chord sequences and routines for the show including a bluesy 'Trouble in Mind' featuring a towering guitar outing by Dominic Ashworth. But, keen though I was to share the stage with our star in the tiny theatre by the sea, I also wanted to make sure that my Half-Dozen were heard too, and suggested that we begin with three tunes before the arrival of the Man on stage.

'Three tunes?' said George with a teasing twinkle in his eye.

'Three short ones,' I said firmly. And from then on, the exchange – even when shortened to 'just two' became a nightly exchange between us.

Our rehearsal was brief but efficient. 'I've not been wasting time,' said George, 'in the meantime. In fact, I've written a book review on the way here. For the *Observer* I think. But I'm looking forward to the concert – and this whole new phase. The only worry is, if it lasts as long as the Feetwarmers, I'll be 106!'

Then it was back to the hotel to change, and when we

arrived back in the downstairs bar there was our newly contracted star in full scarlet and white striped suit with matching hat.

'He looks like a tube of toothpaste!' whispered our drummer Bobby Worth.

Sipping a large Scotch and talking to the landlord, who was plainly enchanted to have such a famous guest behaving in such an approachable manner, George heard nothing. But then Lisa nudged me.

'Don't look now,' she said, 'but his flies are wide open!'

'You tell him!' I said. 'It's OK.' But Lisa didn't want to, so I returned to whisper in his ear. But our star had spotted the problem meantime and was making a small cabaret of putting it right.

'There are three stages to old age,' he announced to his gathering. 'One is forgetting to do your flies up. Two is forgetting to undo them. And three is not giving a damn either way!' The joke would stay in his act for months afterwards.

The show that followed was a huge success, playing to a full house, and later we went to the local pub as our landlord had let us know – kindly if not that hospitably – that there would be no bar facilities at the hotel when we came back. This didn't matter. The pub was called, perhaps with a touch of singularity, the Rumhole, and, like many before and after, had been kept open for George's benefit. He received a hero's welcome in which the band and I basked gloriously and where, to my surprise, the staff would accept Switch cards while I bought a large round. In due course things began to get a little vague and a short lecture by George on Louis Buñuel, the film-noir producer, became gradually more intriguing and bizarre.

'Remarkable film,' said George. 'A man's wife and a whore in the same coffin – and he's wanking over them. Most stimulating I'd say.'

At this point Lisa decided the conversation was a little too surreal for her liking, and strolled over to talk to Dominic and Craig who, with the balance of the Half-Dozen, were keeping a respectable distance from their new friend and feeling slightly mystified as to why – so far – he hadn't bought a welcoming round.

At last, around one o'clock, it was time to return to our hotel and go to bed.

In the morning the Half-Dozen gathered together in the breakfast room to be joined in due course by our star clad only in a colourful nightshirt. A waitress approached his table.

'Would you like coffee or tea, sir?' she enquired.

George thought for a moment. 'I'll have a boiled egg!' he decided.

A ripple of laughter ran around the room.

'Well,' said George, looking pained. 'I really don't see what's so hilarious about a boiled egg.'

Breakfast with our new guest was a delight. Holding court he told tale after tale and, as Bobby Worth observed later there was no need to intrude on the rich Niagara-style monologue of memories that held the attention of the entire room.

'Once,' recalled the Master, 'we were in Wolverhampton in an Indian restaurant, and in comes this huge thug with blood on his face and a bandaged fist and announces "I'm the King of Wolverhampton." He looks across and says, "You're George Melly!" "That's right!" "Well me mum likes you – but I think you're a load of shite." All the time he was perfectly friendly. Then he asked for a bottle of whisky and the waiter said, "We can't serve you, sir – it's after hours."

'"But I'm the King of Wolverhampton."

'So the manager arrives and gives him the bottle of whisky which he drinks – and goes on getting learier until at last he insists on paying. Then he pays again. And then made a hasty exit. After which I caught my train.'

Our first concert – and our first breakfast – were over at last and now it was time for the long drive home. And then, to set to work.

CHAPTER FOUR

Getting on the Record

While the great band changeover was taking place there was a hiatus of four months that autumn while Jack Higgins beavered tirelessly and sometimes vitriolically to relaunch his long-term client in new company. New publicity must be produced, including an expensive and artistic photo session with the Half-Dozen and George for Tom Miller – Jonathan's son – in north London. And the Feetwarmers, with George, completed their last Christmas season at Ronnie's. As Jack's publicity flooded the circuit, it was clear that jobs were coming in at quite a speed. But meantime I was still busy playing one-nighters with the Half-Dozen (including New Year's Eve at the Pizza Express, Maidstone), as well as with the Great British Jazz Band and Don Lusher's Best of British Jazz package, guesting with kindly hosts up and down the country and launching my autobiography *Notes from a Jazz Life* at bookshops in Southend, Bromley and elsewhere.

So that our first job at the Marlowe Theatre Canterbury didn't come round until Wednesday, 22 January 2003, when we appeared as part of Jack Higgins's *Giants of Jazz* spectacular, alongside Kenny Ball and Humphrey Lyttelton and his band. By that time we had four tunes ready – 'Old Rockin' Chair', an up-tempo 'Cakewalkin' Babies from Home', 'Trouble in Mind' featuring Dominic, and a concluding 'The Joint Is Jumpin', with a romping Fats Waller-style piano outing for Craig Milverton.

It was here that I observed for the first time George's pre-show routine. Once his dressing room had been located, the contents of his briefcase – including a packet of Pro-Plus, one of his long-standing liveners – would be laid out with tidy geometric accuracy on the table, his hat nearby and his stage-wear (if different from what he was already wearing) hung on a handy hook.

Our set went well and George was at the top of his form. After an opener from the Half-Dozen, he made his measured way on-stage to sit in an armchair and begin with a stately and dramatic 'Old Rockin' Chair'.

'I open with that,' he explained to the audience, 'as my former signature tune "Goodtime George" written by John Chilton is far less applicable now. People ask me, "What about sex?" I say no! Mind you I've heard they have a new drug in America which combines Viagra with Prozac. So, if you don't get a fuck, you don't give a fuck!'

This produced a roar of laughter and thereafter George had his audience in the palms of both hands. 'Cakewalkin' Babies from Home' followed, on the closing chorus of which George, who sang seated, rose majestically to his feet. 'I only stood up to alarm you!' he said as the song came to an end. Then a dramatic 'Trouble in Mind', a rousing 'The Joint Is Jumpin'' and our part of the show was over.

What I wasn't prepared for was the interval brouhaha that accompanied the sale of CDs and books in the foyer. Lisa, however, was more than equal to the task and, with the help of Susan da Costa, Humphrey Lyttelton's long-time manager and our good friend, we learned quickly how to deal with the queues. While we sold across big trestle tables with a hastily acquired cash float, Humph and George sat well away from the queues, each with a table to himself, signing autographs and chatting with fans. Then it was time for home.

By this time Jack Higgins's high-powered publicity had secured us a healthy level of dates and over the next three months we played the *Giants of Jazz* show at Bedworth, High Wycombe and Truro, as well as solo dates with George at Dudley, Blackburn, Haverhill, Hunstanton, Cambridge, Worcester, and Cole Mathieson's wonderful club, the Concorde at Eastleigh, near Southampton. By now we were getting to know George rather better – often in the course of the long car journeys for which (for an additional payment of £50) we were contracted to pick up the Master, his stagewear and his supplies of merchandise from west London and return him home safely afterwards.

The journeys were entertaining and only hampered by George's increasing deafness which, against the motorway background of a fast car, made conversation virtually impossible. Wide awake and bright-eyed our guest was nevertheless conversationally self-propelling and pleased, at the start of the journey, to entertain his driver and fellow passenger with everything from Max Miller routines to music-hall songs, comedy monologues, jokes and reminiscences of the great and good. An accommodating passenger, he was also happy to stop at motorway services for tea and a light snack (George only ate sparingly), which he would pay for himself before wandering at leisurely speed to buy papers or chocolate. Once back in the car, when conversation was exhausted, he would doze off as we drove.

Sundays could be a different matter, however. Befitting his long career as a journalist, George loved the Sunday papers and regularly brought them all on the way to or from a concert. As every one was a bonus-filled multi-volume affair, he was soon scarcely visible under a mountain of paper, brilliantly coloured Sunday supplements and catalogues, all of which he scanned before delivering the unwanted remains to the front-seat passenger for perusal or disposal. Any pretty girl would be subject to a ritual which I later discovered had been patented by his girlfriend, Babs (not her real name!), whom we were soon to meet. The pin-up girl's most private places would be subject to a jabbing finger and high-pitched 'e-e-e-e-eh' in acknowledgement of the beauties on show, or semi-concealed.

As I had never learned to drive, most of the chauffering fell to Julian, Craig and Dominic Ashworth who, with his usual consideration for others, bought a new car to ensure that his guest was comfortable. Seated in the back of this newly acquired vehicle, George looked around with satisfaction.

'Well, this is very nice,' he said. 'And I haven't shat myself for at least a couple of months now. So everything should be fine.'

Gradually too, we learned about the eccentricities of our guest. 'I was driving George to one job in my brand-new car,' Dominic told me four years later, 'and when he got in he said, "Is it all right to smoke?" I said, "Sure, George, go ahead" and right away he broke my ashtray. It's still in pieces now. And when we got close to our destination I was studying the map and George suddenly broke into some Shakespeare and said, "Do you know what that is?" And while I'm still poring over the map, I said, "Sure, George, it's Shakespeare." And he said, "Yes, of course – but do you know which *play*? Ah-ha, I thought as much. It's *Richard the Second*." And all this time I'm trying to read the map and in a way he's trying to put me down.'

George was seldom if ever malicious, but he was a great teaser as well as being highly observant of our conversation, particularly of any cliché that invaded our talk. His catalogue of remarkable stories and wondrously anarchic adventures demanded acknowledgement rather than conversational exchange. But my obligingly intentioned and usual response of 'Really?' swiftly came under the hammer, returned to me with a particular enthusiasm accompanied by eyebrows disappearing into his greying hair and an exaggerated response to the over-wide smile that I tended to deliver as a visual response to his deafness. George also hated the phrase 'No problem'. This could be awkward as he was regularly inclined to present his minders with small but knotty difficulties and his dismissal of the phrase following their resolution could produce a moment's tension.

He was also inclined to latch on to isolated observations and turn them to permanent visions. Therefore, early on I was branded as eternally hungry for junk food (in fact I'm careful about my bodily intake), unobservant (George unlike me had a quick and perceptive eye for detail of every kind) and ignorant about practically everything apart from jazz. My lack of general art knowledge must have been particularly irritating for him. 'Perhaps you can tell me who painted the *Mona Lisa*?' he once enquired with the hint of a malicious grin. And as, in the heat of the inquisition, I was unable to tell him, he produced the expected wagging finger and disbelieving 'Aaaah . . .' But underneath the occasional teasing which was a lifelong inheritance from the days of Mulligan, then Chilton, George carried a generous heart and early on in our travels frequently brought treats with him including, on one occasion, quails' eggs, a delicacy which he much enjoyed and had previously recommended to his fellow travellers. The contents of this large and delicious bagful he shared with his driver and fellow passenger, covering poor Dominic Ashworth's rear seat with shell and salt.

Very early on, however, he discovered my interest in erotic

art. 'Do you like cunt? Or fucking? Then next time I shall have something for you.' And he did – an edition of *Erotic Review* – later followed up by several more, for which he would give me his considered (and valued) opinion on what was genuinely erotic and what constituted 'just pin-up pictures really'.

George was blissfully ignorant of the motorways of Britain, but not averse to holding court at inappropriate moments. And the strain on the navigator – purposely and visibly perusing a map while attempting to respond positively to conversation from the rear – could be considerable. Nick Millward, our resilient and ever good-humoured drummer in later years, often became George's driver, and quickly got his number, recognising that, once his passenger was any more than a mile from Shepherd's Bush, his knowledge of navigation was rudimentary at best. This seldom stopped him offering helpful hints, however, which Nick skilfully learned to field.

'I think if you'd taken that little left turn off the Uxbridge Road we'd easily have been home by now . . .'

'George – don't start!' As we were rounding Blackheath, ten miles or more from the Uxbridge Road, the reproof was justified.

Nick also learned to deal with George's deafies without in any way causing offence.

'What kind of car is this?'

'Diesel.'

'Easel?'

'DIESEL' (louder this time).

'Threesome?'

'Diesel, you silly old deaf twat!'

As time went on other more serious hazards than deafness or eccentric efforts at navigation would raise their heads. But that was later.

In contrast to his social eccentricities off the stand, George was one of the most receptive musicians I had ever encountered. Blissfully ignorant of technical matters such as keys, he was happy to sing whatever he found on the typed programme placed on the music stand next to his rocking chair. As well as selecting repertoire, which rapidly settled into a working programme, I was to set tempii, direct solos and indicate when my new colleague was due to come back in. Perhaps it was the receptive and empathetic side of George that enjoyed direction. And very regularly he would announce to the audience that he'd joined our band, apparently unaware – or at least unconcerned – that it was very much the other way round. We had joined George Melly. And now we were working!

At this point record producer Peter Clayton raised his ever-enthusiastic head. Peter (not to be confused with the late and much-missed broadcaster) was a highly successful builder in South London with music in his heart and a new company called Robinwood Productions. We'd become great friends when Len Skeat had invited me to become involved in a Robinwood project – unlikely on the face of it – to bring jazz and dancing back to the Albert Hall. To do this Peter had hired the Hall and three British groups – Keith Nichols' Cotton Club Band, Kenny Ball and his Jazzmen, singer Carla Valenti, compere Nicky Martin and an all-star line up, which I was to lead and included Dave Shepherd, Tommy Whittle, Roy Williams, Roger Nobes, John Pearce, Len and the great drummer Ronnie Verrell. I was far from sure that even a bill that packed with homegrown talent could fill Britain's biggest concert hall but Peter was adamant that it could. He advertised his concert in a slew of periodicals (right down to the *Women's Institute Journal*) and, to my amazement, later in the year, on the night of 23 September, we walked out to face over three thousand people. For good measure Peter recorded the whole thing and issued it on a double CD *Ragtime to Swing recorded live at the Royal Albert Hall.*

'Well,' said Peter one morning, 'how do you feel about an album with George and the Half-Dozen?'

'Is a frog watertight?' I said delightedly and we set to work.

The first matter was to put Peter, the enthusiastic newcomer, in touch with Jack Higgins, the weathered veteran, and Jack drove a professional bargain. We were to record at Clownspocket Studios, in Bexley, run by tenorist Derek Nash in mid-April. George was to be housed for three nights in the five-star Marriott Hotel nearby; the Half-Dozen were to receive full union rates for three days' recording and I was to receive an extra sum for writing arrangements. Peter was to produce the album, an excellent idea as he has a natural ear for what's good or not, how a mix should sound and even how an arrangement might be fashioned.

This talent had already come in handy. In early March, Peter had come to see me play at Grantham Jazz Festival with Don Rendell, a local rhythm section and, most remarkably, a young pianist-singer called Jamie Cullum. Rather to our surprise Jamie really didn't want to play on our set and was reluctant to read Don's arrangements. 'I normally do my own stuff,' he said self-effacingly and did. Playing a roaring trio set following Don and I, he set light to the room playing driving piano (seated and standing), singing up a storm and playing drums on the piano-top like an intellectual Jerry Lee Lewis. At the point in his show when he included a rock-beat 'It Ain't Necessarily So', Peter nudged me.

'You know, Dig,' he said. 'George should do "Frankie and Johnny" like that . . .'

So, with manuscript paper, pencils, sharpener and erasers at the ready, I set to work at Lisa's piano writing. George and I had talked through tunes and, true to his Bessie Smith roots, he wanted to recreate 'On Revival Day' and 'Trombone Chollie' but left most of the remaining choices to me. He was receptive to almost all my ideas: 'Not exactly one of my favourites . . . but, if you want, I'll sing it of course.' So I had a clean creative slate and my idea was to re-present some old Melly standards, including 'Funny Feathers' from the Mick Mulligan days, 'Dr Jazz' and 'Michigan Water Blues', with material less familiar to Melly lovers, including 'I Can't Get Started with You', 'Sugar' and 'September Song'. Once the creative blister was broken, the ideas came thick and fast. The Half-Dozen is an enormously creative unit which can tackle anything from high-class Dixieland to electric jazz-fusion. So 'Frankie and Johnny' could come with a rock-beat and Herbie Hancock's 'Chameleon' riff. 'The Joint Is Jumpin' could encompass a driving tenor-riff borrowed from Wardell Gray and Dexter Gordon. 'All the Girls Go Crazy' could re-adopt the basic New Orleans riffs built into the original, then progress to a jump-band conclusion. 'I Can't Get Started with You' could incorporate the under-heard verse with a salute to vintage trumpet-master Bunny Berigan (as well as Bing Crosby and Rosemary Clooney). And 'September Song' would make an appropriate closing track. I was excited, and so was Peter.

So finally the session days arrived. George had been installed in his hotel the night before and I had lodged with my producer. The day was bright and clear as we drove to the Marriott Hotel to be greeted at its palatial reception.

'We've come to collect Mr Melly,' Peter explained.

A cloud passed over the receptionist's face. 'Ah,' she said, 'I think you might need to go up. There's a slight problem.'

And there was. George was flat on his back in his nightshirt, motionless on the bed groaning with pain. A nearby wastebin had been used as a pee-pot.

'I went to the bathroom in the night,' he said, 'and slipped on the floor. I managed to crawl back to bed but now I can't move.'

'Should we call an ambulance?' I suggested.

'No!' cried George fortissimo, the wounded hero. 'I'm determined to do the sessions. But I shall need a wheelchair and quite a lot of help I daresay.'

The fall had cracked several ribs. But the resourceful Peter, a trained nurse in former years, managed to hoist George upright amid yells of discomfort while I went in search of a wheelchair. Once Melly was seated Peter was able to divest him of his nightshirt, revealing a body badly infected with eczema and psoriasis, and finally managed to recloak him in an ornate if slightly brief kaftan. With our star upright in his wheelchair we made our stately yet spectacular way to the foyer where a cab owned by a friend of Peter's awaited us and drove through Bexley and up the hill to Clownspocket Studios.

Over the next two days with Derek Nash we recorded eighteen tracks, George alternately seated in the recording booth to record guide vocals and the big garden outside, urbanely smoking and enjoying the garden views while the Half-Dozen toiled inside. To fortify myself against the pressures of recording I had brought a litre bottle of fine Russian vodka, a gift from friends in the Midlands and was mildly dismayed to find that at the end of day one it was almost gone, making regular trips to Sandy Nash's generously stocked bar a necessity. The ebullient Sandy made trips in return to the studio providing sandwiches, tea, coffee and stronger beverages as required, while Derek worked his miracles at the desk. At the end of the day, George was driven back to the hotel where a group of young tough south Londoners recognised him in the bar and encircled him to gossip and drink.

On the third day it was time to ensure that all George's vocal tracks were laid down for editing and tuning purposes and this was a warm April. In the booth, tiny in any case, George, Peter, Derek and myself gathered for an intensive day's work in a warm and airless space. The regular use of a pee-bottle intensified what was already a funky atmosphere and it was hard to miss the equipment that had carried George through so many triumphant physical encounters.

The following week we had been due to mix the Melly album, to be called, like Jack Higgins's new show, *Singing and Swinging the Blues*. But the ever-generous Peter had liked what he heard of the Half-Dozen in-studio and rededicated the three reserved days to recording what was to be our new band album called *Things Ain't What They Used To Be*. The mixing turned out well, and we had fun, particularly with 'Frankie and Johnny', which turned into a full-blown production with spectacular guitar from Dominic Ashworth recalling both Duane Eddy and Jimi Hendrix, plus electronic brass-stab gunshots, and shouts of alarm when Frankie's 44 rooty-toot-tooted Johnny into eternity.

George recovered quickly and, by the end of April, was ready to travel up with me up by train to Barrow-in-Furness for a quartet date, then down with the Half-Dozen to another *Giants of Jazz* show in Halifax. Both shows had 'sold out' signs up when we arrived.

Later George explained to me why the bathroom accident had occurred. Along with other increasing medication he had been prescribed water pills, necessitating regular nightly trips to the bathroom, a miserable experience making prolonged sleep virtually impossible. It also meant that − in the old phrase − when he had to go, he had to go.

'Once,' he said, 'I was taken short and had to find a nearby wall in Shepherd's Bush. Which I did. But then I felt a police-man's hand on my shoulder. "What's all this, then?" I explained that I was taking water pills and that peeing when it happened was an urgent necessity. "Oh very well, sir," said the policeman. "But perhaps next time you could find an alternative to the wall of our police station?'"

CHAPTER FIVE

Travelling Shoes and Blues

By the spring of 2003 Jack Higgins's publicity had paid off and by British jazz standards we were working very hard indeed. Seldom did a week go by without at least one or two concerts, and our show – tidied up further by the arrangements we'd recorded for our new album – began to turn into a smooth but high-powered presentation. It was also much the same most nights, a point that bothered me as George, in a previous life with Mick Mulligan, had been known to complain about singing most of the same songs night after night. But at this point he didn't seem to mind.

Consequently, our first half more or less permanently comprised George's new opener 'Old Rockin' Chair' with some exchanged business between George and I ('My Cane's By My Side', 'And a Fine Upstanding Thing!', 'Was . . . !'), 'Cakewalkin' Babies', a heavily blues-soaked 'Trouble in Mind' (featuring Dominic's Claptonesque flat guitar) and usually 'Sweet Georgia Brown' as a closer. Then, on our second half, George would return for a solo on 'Michigan Water Blues' (with Craig Milverton's solo piano) before 'Dr Jazz', a ballad such as 'Gee Baby Ain't I Good to You' or the defiant 'Tain't Nobody's Bizness If I Do', a jumping 'All the Girls Go Crazy' (complete with the song's original words later on celebrating 'All the Whores Go Crazy 'bout the Way I Ride') and, to finish with, a romping 'The Joint Is Jumpin', featuring Craig's marvellous solo piano at high speed, with exchanges between Len Skeat and Bobby Worth before the end. The encore inevitably was 'Nuts'. 'Can you imagine waking up in the morning,' George would muse to his audiences in mock-envy, 'and remembering "I'm Roosevelt 'The Honeydripper' Sykes?"' For this finale the lights were turned up on the audience and George would pick out the unfortunate man 'whose shirt is blue/he's got very big nuts; he just don't know what to do', 'whose shirt is peach/he's got very nice nuts but his arms don't reach', before turning the joke on himself: 'See this man – he's big and fat/they say that his nuts are no bigger than that' (not true as we knew) and finally, 'See this man/his head is bald/they say he ain't got no nuts at all.' It was a marvellous show.

And we were busy! George's datesheet with the Feetwarmers had been slackening, as we knew, but now he was back and doing well. Over the next few months we played the *Giants of Jazz* package – three-header shows co-starring Humphrey Lyttelton and either Kenny Ball or Acker Bilk – in Halifax, Coventry and Bath. In early May, we played in Derry at the Millennium Forum, a superb new building where one of our company (though not one of the Half Dozen) trashed his hotel room in a rare moment of hotel rage, rock'n'roll style.

We also took George, with a cut-down quartet, Feetwarmers' style, to Brighton and, with the full band again, to Hertford, Tunbridge Wells and George's home town of Liverpool. Here we played at the tiny Neptune Theatre, distinguished by its lack of a ground-floor entrance (you can only get to its charming first-floor auditorium via a lift) and by the fact that our star had made his first-ever on-stage appearance there as a child. We also played Ludlow, Bracknell, Hever Castle, Aboyne, Southend and Whitstable.

By May our new album *Singing and Swinging the Blues* had been mastered, the artwork completed and the generous sixteen-page booklet adorned with a blessing from George's friend Sir Paul McCartney. George had written to Holly Dearden, Paul's secretary, and received a delightful answer from the man himself, stating that he'd known George since his days in Liverpool when he was already a legend on the jazz music scene, and had followed his career since then, describing George as 'a lovely man'.

Such a coup meant a lot to Peter Clayton. As well as printing the words within the booklet he had a sticker printed to be attached to the cellophane wrapper of the CD. A fine piece of advertising, but George had difficulties grasping the fact that you could read Paul's words both in the booklet and on the sticker on the CD's disposable wrapping. 'Stupid!' he snorted. 'A total waste! Unwrap the damn thing and all my hard work – and Paul's – goes straight in the rubbish! What an IDIOT.' We never quite managed to get the point across.

When the CD was finally ready to go to press, Peter, as ever awash with enthusiasm and excitement, decided that we should take it to George's house for a ceremonial debut and play-through. This turned out to be a distinct anticlimax. Very few musicians enjoy hearing their own work anyhow – especially just over 65 minutes of it. And Peter's exuberance failed to receive the reception it deserved. Diana Melly, who was long experienced in the arrival of new recordings, asked for it to be played at moderate volume, which meant that George couldn't hear it at all, even if he had been hugely interested. Grand-daughter Kezzie wandered in and out of the kitchen-diner in search of boiled eggs rather than music, and the two producers sat in increasing discomfort before a quick and tactful exit seemed the best choice.

In mid-August at Whitstable – the very pretty town on the Kent coast famous for its oysters – we were to be joined by our agent and champion Jack Higgins who had announced his intention of coming to see our two shows, a rare occurrence for him. I had yet to get to know Jack well and, like many of his clients, was still terrified of him. My concerns were doubled by the fact that the Half-Dozen's guitarist, Dominic Ashworth, had let me know some time before that he would be on holiday during the two dates and, as we could play quite happily with just piano, bass and drums and earn a little more money too, I had failed to let Jack know.

I knew he would almost certainly be furious. But to tell him in advance would be bound to provoke a row. With heart in mouth and nails bitten to their quicks, I approached the dates, ready to face the thunderstorm I felt sure would ensue. Finally the day arrived and down we travelled to Whitstable to be told that Mr Higgins had checked into his hotel and would join us at the theatre. So, with just six men and our star, we took the stage and when the set was over I steeled myself for an ugly row in the making.

In the dressing room, there was Jack – broad-shouldered, distinguished, immaculately dressed in jacket, tailored slacks, shirt and cravat, talking to Len Skeat. I tried to make myself invisible in the curtains but to no avail. With measured tread, Jack approached me.

'One short, eh?' he enquired briefly.

'Yes,' I stammered. 'I'm sorry I didn't say anything . . . I was afraid it might spoil the weekend . . .'

Jack cut in. 'Tell me next time!' he said. 'Otherwise we might have complaints. And we don't want that. Now

– tomorrow, you, Lisa and George will be my guests at the best restaurant in Whitstable. Is one o'clock convenient?'

Of course it was. My merciful agent had decided that this was to be a happy weekend devoid of rows. And next day, with him, we feasted on a seafood lunch of incomparable quality, oysters and all.

Only our hotel, well away from Whitstable centre, cast a shadow on the proceedings. An inflexible landlady (definitely one of the old school) offered no hot water after 9 a.m. and almost nothing in the way of hospitality. Chris Gower took his revenge at breakfast-time by wandering morosely around the garden, then being sick into a handy flowerbed. But on day two there was a break in the clouds. The Half-Dozen and I were cheered to find that Dave Gelly, jazz critic of the *Observer*, had voted *Singing and Swinging the Blues* his Record of the Week. Generous as always, Lisa bought seven copies of the paper and we celebrated in the hotel car park listening to our new work of art on her in-car CD player. George was proud of his latest achievement too, and for many months thereafter worked a reference to our triumph into his show.

'Our new CD,' he would say, 'has been voted by the *Observer*'s jazz critic as his Record of the Week. All the more remarkable, as the man concerned usually only likes the kind of modern jazz I refer to as the fire-in-a-petshop brand.' The term refers to the kind of modern jazz known as 'free' but by its detractors as 'squeaky-bonk'. But Dave Gelly, a commentator who not only knows jazz from its beginning to the contemporary but also plays elegant and expert tenor in the style of Lester Young, would have been rightfully dismayed by such an inappropriate dismissal.

We were now settling into a show proper. Lisa's presence at the shows was invaluable, not only for her solid support for a project with which she was increasingly familiar, but also for her help with the new and demanding matter of 'produce'. Now we had a new album to sell as well as the subsequent issue of our own new album on Robinwood *Things Ain't What They Used To Be* (with George as special guest on one favourite track of mine, the old Eddie Cantor song 'When My Ship Comes In'). The two albums were joined by George's liberal bibliography, including his Penguin trilogy (*Scouse Mouse*, *Rum, Bum and Concertina* and *Owning Up*) and a wonderfully eccentric account of his fishing passions and encounters (at least one of them, literally sexual) called *Hooked*.

Before a show, while George settled himself into his dressing room, arranging his bagful of accoutrements with geometric precision as usual, it was our job to carry in boxes of books and CDs, locate the house manager, establish what if any percentage of sales was to be taken by the house and then set up two tables: one for the books and records and one nearby at which George would sign autographs. CDs must be stripped of their cellophane covers for autograph purposes, books unpacked and the quantity of produce counted and listed. A float of twenty or thirty pounds must be brought or located on-site, and sheets of paper plus felt-tipped pen left at George's table for admirers to write down their names if he was too deaf to hear them. Then the produce itself must be set out attractively and covered with a protective tablecloth to avoid preshow theft.

At half-time, shows frequently resembled a beer-garden. Queues of people would make for our stand, skilfully run by Lisa but usually accompanied by the bandleader, sweating from the efforts of his first set, straight from the bandstand into the arms of the crowd. This wasn't fun and, if Lisa couldn't be there, was liable to turn into a chaotic nightmare of hurried financial exchanges, inebriated recording of sales and the promise to return after an interval devoid of rest, to the second half of our show. This bewildering business undoubtedly led me nearer to the bottle of vodka I normally carried with me and occasionally to later bouts of frustration and ill-temper as, having completed a sell-out concert, it would be necessary to run back to the stall, complete the sales, report on them to the house manager, sign receipts and (worst of all) calculate percentages owed plus or minus VAT before returning a shade hazily to the dressing room. There I would attend to the small matters of packing trumpet and mutes, gathering music and paying my patient friends in the Half-Dozen who would help in dismantling and packing our own PA away, minus their perspiring leader.

And this wasn't all the clerking involved. Once home with recorded sales and a bag of money it was Lisa's and my job to rationalise figures (often at odds with the scribbled sales accounting on the paper) and then pay the money into George's two companies. 'Man Woman and Bulldog' for records and 'Wing Commander Jack' (named after Diana Melly, known as the 'Winco' by George and Jack Higgins) for books. For these unpaid tasks Lisa rightly asked for a commission of £1 for each CD sold, but it was small return for the work involved.

Later on I took on paymaster's duties single-handed and one day a bright-eyed young counter clerk questioned me.

'We've been wondering,' she said, 'about Man Woman and Bulldog. It's a funny name for a company. What does it mean?'

Modesty forbade me – certainly at 10 a.m. one Monday morning – from explaining that 'Man Woman and Bulldog' was one of George's favoured party-pieces. Baring his bottom he would advance into the room backwards and bent double revealing those swarthy balls and a mighty penis. 'Man.' Then a return appearance with penis and testicles pulled forward between his legs. 'Woman.' And finally – with balls only to view – 'Bulldog'!

About now, however, serious challenges were raising their threatening heads for our star. Following his cracked ribs prior to our first recording dates, George had remained in pain for a while and become depressed. A general check-up had involved an x-ray and this revealed a shadow on his lung. The scan that followed produced a chilling diagnosis: lung cancer, a verdict that devastated Diana Melly. A biopsy had been offered but George, fearful of needles and the threat that an operation might interrupt or even finish his singing career, decided that he might go out the way he had chosen to live: by drinking, smoking and living the life he loved. These days Diana was often away from home on holiday or at the Mellys' cottage in Bagnor but now comforted herself with counselling and the acquisition of two papillon dogs, Bobby and Joey (quickly and appropriately christened by George the 'yap-yaps'). She then hired a homehelp, a handsome Zimbabwean called Desdemona. George's 77th birthday in August approached with plans for a big party – a joy-week at Bagnor to which a succession of friends would visit, including Mick and Tessa Mulligan and playwright Julian Mitchell. The week was a great success but a month later a second x-ray revealed that the tumour had disappeared. The Reaper, it seemed, had sheathed his scythe.

(Above) George was guest of honour with the Half Dozen at the first Hayne Barton Jazz Festival just outside Exeter in 2004 where he shared some happy blues with Val Wiseman, another of Britain's great jazz singers and star of her own *Lady sings the Blues* show. (David J. Thomas)

(Left) George prior to one of our first gigs together in 2003 – a natural for the camera at any time, even when making for the dressing room with a whiskey. In the background is Dominic Ashworth who had found a secluded spot to warm up before the concert.

'He's the bon vivant you want', as Johnny Mercer would have put it. George, with ciggy, relaxing in style in the dressing room at Ronnie Scott's, in one of his famous suits – the perfect way to be recognised wherever you go.

(Above) Two old brothers in arms – Mick Mulligan came to see George every Christmas at Ronnie's and here George is reminding Mick that it's his round.

(Below) Outside Ronnie Scott's for our first Christmas season. Left to right: Digby, Julian Marc Stringle, George, Dominic Ashworth, Chris Gower, Bobby Worth, Craig Milverton, Len Skeat.

On the way to a gig, relaxing outside a friendly pub, in another of those great suits (and ties) – the eye-patch was cosmetic by the way – and just out of shot is a cup of tea. Definitely a first!

George Melly, resplendent in kaftan, standing up for the final chorus of 'Cakewalkin' Babies'. 'I only stood up to alarm you!' he would say before returning to his chair. (David J. Thomas)

By the time we worked with him George always sat down to perform and here he is, immaculate as always from top to toe, on stage at the Upton-on-Severn Jazz Festival 2006 with Craig, Digby and Dominic Ashworth giving out with some technicolour blues.

(Above) Two old friends (with a very friendly waiter) sharing a joke; George with Humphrey Lyttelton at the Beaulieu Jazz Festival fiftieth anniversary concert, August 2006.

(Below) George and Digby at the Bulls Head for the last time in February, 2007. George is explaining that Alan Yentob hasn't been filling in his lottery numbers.

(Above) At the George Melly testimonial concert, 100 Oxford Street, in June 2007. It was George's last public appearance. Left to right: Julian Marc Stringle, Digby, Dominic Ashworth, Len Skeat. (www.edmacphoto.co.uk)

(Below) 'One more time!' – Diana Melly cues George for the last song of his career at the testimonial concert. (www.edmacphoto.co.uk)

CHAPTER SIX

Ronnie's and Beyond

In October, we played a concert at the Mercury Theatre, Colchester, where George had collapsed and been rushed to hospital some years before. This time there was little fear of that and our star received a standing ovation.

It was also at this time that I endured my first fully fledged fight with Jack Higgins. The day of the concert he had rung with the offer of some work in Somerset.

'But,' growled Jack, 'you'd better get your act together. Because there's word down there that Digby Fairweather is unreliable.'

'Oh,' I joked, 'another paternity summons? I'll see to it, Jack.' But the remark rankled.

The next morning Jack rang again. 'Who took the cheque last night?'

'Lisa did,' I said. 'The manager gave it to her and we're posting it off today.'

'How many times,' said Jack, his voice rising in a crescendo of fury, 'do I have to make it clear to you that the cheque comes direct to me. Get your act together. And tell your fucking girlfriend to do the same.'

I held my breath, then let go of my temper. 'Listen, Jack,' I said, watching myself say the words, my breath now catching in fury. 'First, you don't speak to me like that! Second, you never speak of my partner in such terms again. And, while we're on the subject, I want to know who it is that accused me of unreliability?'

'What are you fucking talking about?'

'You know as well as I do, Jack! I want to know exactly who said it. Then I shall ring them and demand an apology or they'll hear from my solicitor for character defamation.'

The voice at the other end became apoplectic. 'You little bastard! You don't get involved with my clients!'

'Oh yes, I do,' I said, 'if they slander me! Now get off the phone and call back when you've brought some courtesy back to your voice.'

There was dead silence. Then, 'You won't be hearing from me!' said a flat voice. Click.

Christ, I thought, as I stood shaking with the receiver still in my hand. That might just be it! Plainly, heavyweight fighting was now on the cards.

But not for long. Later on, Jack and I became good working partners and friends. But, as I was now finding out, he could and would take a row to its limits if necessary as part of his professional regime. Any ensuing anger would dissipate and sometimes be forgotten altogether within a few days, or resolved with a quick reconciliatory exchange. Only his clients were sometimes left with their emotions in tatters; at least until they learned the ropes with their irascible (but arguably incomparable) agent. Most of his other clients feared Jack too, including that true gentleman of the profession, trombonist Don Lusher, who had spent over fifty years at the top. Now, under his immaculately pressed suit, he was worried in his heart about the decreasing lack of work for his package the Best of British Jazz in which I had taken Kenny Baker's place after his death in 1999. One day he rang Jack to talk about it.

'Jack! Good morning to you. Don Lusher here. I was ringing to ask you whether perhaps things are a little slow for the Best of British Jazz just now?'

'Slow? Slow?' I was told that Jack had responded, his voice rising. 'Of course they're slow! First of all, you're too old. Second, there are no fucking stars left in your band. And three, have you read page 27 of today's *Daily Telegraph*?'

'No,' admitted the quaking Don.

'Well, read it! And you'll see an article proving that the trombone is the most unpopular instrument in Britain today. So that's why you're not getting any fucking work. Goodbye!' Click.

But Jack was never above telling a story against himself. Once, while running European International Artistes from his prestigious office in Charing Cross Road, he called an errant bandleader in for a head-to-head bollocking. Later, he walked down Charing Cross Road and dropped into the magnificent public toilet that still welcomes visitors to its palatial depths. On the marbled walls, Jack told me with a chuckle, he read an expansive piece of black-ink graffiti: 'There's only one bigger shithouse in London than this and that's Jack Higgins.'

A few days later Jack rang me again, this time with a big offer. 'You'll be playing Ronnie Scott's this Christmas! For three weeks starting Monday, 15 December. The pay is £75 a night per musician . . . no bonus on New Year's Eve. And you'll just have Christmas Eve and Christmas Day off. Tell the boys!'

I couldn't contain my delight. Never had I played at the legendary Ronnie's and, of course, neither had the Half-Dozen. Everyone was thrilled and Julian heroically declared himself able to finish his Christmas pantomime at the Chicken Shed Theatre in north London and then accelerate down to the club in time for our first set at 10.45 p.m.

'The hours are killing,' warned my old friend Len Skeat, a veteran at Ronnie's. 'You'll have to watch yourself.'

And, as we would find out, Ronnie's timetable made a wreck of our body clocks. The first set ran for an hour until 11.45; the second, from 1 a.m. until 2. I thought we could cope with this but two problems haunted me: the acoustics at Ronnie's (incredibly dead) and that vexatious matter of no New Year's Eve bonus. Most musicians at the time reckoned to make at least £200–£300 for turning out to welcome the New Year in. But this was not to be and negotiation with its taciturn manager Pete King was an impossibility. Even Jack Higgins had reached an impasse of non-communication with him: two heavyweights in an immovable clinch.

As usual it was Lisa who came up with the answer. Pay the musicians £70 a night, she suggested, and save the extra for a New Year's Eve bonus. Good idea! Every member of the Half-Dozen would appear to receive a double fee on the night. This harmless bit of financial adjustment satisfied everyone (including me) and a sound check with Miles Ashton on the afternoon of our first night proved that masterly Miles (the son of Bill Ashton MBE, founder of the National Youth Jazz Orchestra) knew how to make us all sound good. On that first night the club was almost full and by night three the 'house full' signs were up for good; queues were forming in an orderly manner along Frith Street to pass under the somewhat formidable gaze of the house staff, a genial giant, Monty, a deeply dignified and immaculately dressed accomplice who hovered in the foyer like a taciturn ghost, and several other heavies for good measure.

'Leave the CDs with us,' we were instructed but Lisa wasn't having any. 'Look,' she said, 'they're just hidden behind on that rack and nobody's selling anything! I'll do it.' Which she did, determinedly setting up a stall in the downstairs bar and selling like a champion. John Chilton had always fulsomely tipped the front-of-house heavies (and I might have done the same) but once again down-to-earth Lisa came to the rescue. 'They're not doing anything,' she pointed out. 'Why should they get a tip?' Which was exactly right. Lisa's sales desk was a hive of activity night after night and she made a great deal of money for Man Woman and Bulldog and Wing Commander Jack. At the end she offered Pete King commission but behind that taciturn tough exterior there beat a kindly heart and Pete didn't take any money at all, beyond a token £50 for the use of the table. On New Year's Eve he even invaded our band room with bottles of champagne and the deathless greeting: 'I suppose I'd better say "fucking Happy New Year"!'

One night at Ronnie's, while making our way through 'Trouble in Mind', I became aware of a high-pitched voice. 'Goody Goody!'

It was quite a job for anyone to make themselves heard against the thundering roar of Dominic Ashworth's marvellous blues-soaked guitar, but someone was managing it. And then again, 'Goody Goody!' higher still, and nearer.

Suddenly, vaguely, I was aware of a formidable figure invading the stage to my left, only to be headed gently but firmly off by my kindly trombone player Chris Gower. As he escorted the stranger out of harm's way, the cry of 'Goody Goody' was as audible as ever.

The mysterious invader turned out to be Babs. Tall, with ravishingly slim legs, a full and fair face and figure and an enchanting smile (when we could see her). Babs was George's closest female friend after Diana and the two of them were firm enemies. Diana well knew of her existence and she remained the most visible threat to domestic harmony in the Melly household. Very drunk indeed on this night, Babs unexpectedly turned up in the dressing room the next night and enchanted us all with her smile and a card of apology which was one of the rudest I'd ever seen.

For the next few years she was a frequent visitor to George's shows and one of these – at the Bull's Head in Barnes – produced a first for the Half-Dozen. Deeply committed to a passionate blues trumpet solo amid the roar of sound that the Half-Dozen could produce, I was vaguely aware of suppressed snorts of laughter from Len Skeat and Bobby Worth. Opening my eyes at the end I saw Babs in the front row. Enfolded in the swirling heat of the music she had raised her skirt to waist height, celebrating her uncovered and glorious femininity for all to see. Having on previous occasions ripped off my T-shirt at the climax of a blues while touring with Carole Clegg's blues band Speakeasy, I appreciated the passion of the moment and all that was necessary was to nod and throw an appreciative smile at Babs' beautiful and generous womanhood.

George was regularly attended by droves of fans at Ronnie's, many of whom I was vaguely aware that I should know. Diana Melly made a rare and welcome appearance. So did the highly celebrated Maggie Hambling, whose wonderfully perceptive three-dimensional portrait of George hangs in the National Gallery, whose sculpture stands proud on the beach at Snape and whose brilliant drawings adorned his last book *Slowing Down*. Unfortunately, I didn't recognise the figure who threw a critical glance at me in the downstairs bar at Ronnie's and declared, 'Your band's too loud.'

I've always defended my band to the hilt and was proud of every member, so criticism from a stranger was dangerous territory at any time.

'Which particular pieces – and perhaps which bars – are you thinking of?'

'It's just too damned loud. That's all!'

'Well, in that case,' I said, 'I suggest you make your way to some music that pleases you better!' At least, that's roughly what I suggested.

Later George came to the rescue as usual. 'That was Maggie,' he said. 'She's a very old – and very good – friend of mine. And a great artist. But of course she was a bit tipsy. And I've rung her up and told her off.'

That was typical of George. Always loyal to friends but non-judgemental, he was a great peace-maker except when roused beyond endurance. So the next time I met Maggie – after the publication of *Slowing Down* I extended a hand and said, 'I thought your cartoons for *Slowing Down* were wonderful.'

'They're sketches,' said Miss Hambling forcibly, 'not cartoons.' And quite right too. Oh well.

CHAPTER SEVEN

Ribs, Gags and Rows

For the first four weeks of January 2004 the Half-Dozen, George and I readjusted our body clocks and made ourselves busy. Very little happens for musicians in January while the world is paying off its Christmas bills and, apart from one appearance at the Pizza Express, Maidstone, with my quartet and an early concert with George at St Albans, things were quiet until the very last day of January. But then, at the Chequer Mead Theatre, East Grinstead, things took a dramatic turn.

The stall had been set up in the foyer, the sound check completed and our first half had gone well. A full theatre, a high and imposing stage, good sound and a band that by now was as tight as a sailor's knot. But after our first half, and our opening two tunes for the second ('Two short ones?' George had teased me, as usual, before we went on), he was nowhere to be seen. While I improvised a blues, Julian went in search of him and found our star gently contemplating life and his vision in the dressing-room mirror, all his usual accoutrements beneath his reflective gaze.

Julian brought him back to the stage and our second half thereafter went as smoothly as ever. After 'Nuts' George raised himself to take a bow and, over the microphone, I called for renewed applause for the man who, in John Chilton's handy phrase, was ever 'the funniest of the wise men and wisest of the funny men'. As George moved forward to bow again, I turned my head past him to wave for applause for 'our great drummer, Bobby Worth'. But within the second the applause abruptly vanished like the terminal swipe of a sword into hushed silence. I looked back and George was nowhere to be seen. Where could he be? Then I looked down beyond the stage and there he was lying motionless eight feet below on the floor of the auditorium.

My God, I thought, he's dead . . .

From the auditorium people rushed forward as the Half-Dozen made its confused way off-stage. By the time we were alongside, George's eyes were open. But could he move? What might be broken? His legs? His spine?

But to a round of applause he was hauled to his feet and, supported by staunch fans, made his way out and sat down determinedly at the sale table while an ambulance was called. This amazing man refused to be cowed and chatted amiably with concerned audience members while Lisa, at his side, did a roaring trade in CDs and books. Finally the ambulance men arrived.

'Bloody 'ell!' said one. 'It's George Melly! 'Ere! Can you sign one of those books for me?'

'Come on, Joe,' said the other one, 'we've got to get this man into hospital.'

Which in due course they did. Lisa and I followed the ambulance and, after a prolonged wait on a stretcher in the Accident and Emergency department, George was pronounced fit to go. We drove him home and put him to bed, arriving back as dawn broke. But it was Sunday.

So I phoned Diana in the country. She in turn phoned George who, by now, was in a lot of pain; he had broken his collarbone and his ribs were badly bruised. Diana dialled 999 for an ambulance and George went to hospital again and was later discharged. But he had damaged himself and for the time being had to sleep in a tall-backed chair in his sitting-room. He was also unable to fish, became sadder for a while and, according to Diana, grumpy for the first time. The hospital's offer to set his collarbone was refused – despite the fact that one shoulder would end up higher than the other – and it was five months before our star could pick up his rod and line again. During this time he had what used to be called a 'turn': wandering in a confused way around his house, trying to make a bed up in his kitchen, and talking of seeing things that weren't there; a hallucinatory result, said the doctor, of too many pills and whisky together.

But on-stage our resilient star refused to show any more signs of wear and tear. During February we played Blackpool, the delightful theatres at Richmond (transformed, for the great film *Topsy-Turvey*, celebrating Gilbert and Sullivan's *Mikado*, into a re-created Savoy Theatre) and Camberley. On the way back from this concert, with George doing his best to get comfortable in the back of Lisa's car, we unexpectedly found ourselves running on a flat tyre and hauled our way into a side road to consider the situation.

Ever practical – and realising that neither George nor I was fully equipped to change the wheel – Lisa went in search of a garage, while I rang the AA.

'Hello. I'm afraid we have a flat and no one to change it. Can you send someone out?'

'Certainly. What's the name?'

'Bridgey,' I said, 'Lisa Bridgey.' There was a long pause.

'I'm sorry, sir, we don't have that name on our records.'

'Yes, you do,' I said irritably, 'I'm sure!'

At this point Lisa came back and took the phone, just in time. 'I'm sorry,' she said and handed the phone back to me. 'I'm not in the AA. I'm in National Recovery. Call them and I'll try the garage down the road.'

I hadn't heard of National Recovery but, in a gentle haze, dialled Directory Enquiries and asked to be put through.

'Hello,' said a steady and cultivated female voice. 'This is National Rescue. Are you at sea or at shore?'

'Excuse me?'

'This is National Rescue. Are you at sea or at shore?'

'I'm in Sevenoaks,' I said, by now thoroughly confused. But there, once again, was Lisa who averted the potential oncoming swarms of helicopters and fleets of lifesaving craft by setting the records (and the phonecall) straight. While off I went to buy kebabs for my long-suffering driver and guest, who was languishing in his back seat and nursing ribs that were still sore.

But travelling in-car with George was becoming less fun than it had been. To begin with I'd been delighted that he was prepared to travel with his musicians, rather than taking a star's solitary train journey, but George was gregarious by nature and completely happy (as Diana had assured me from the start) to be with friends in the car. The diminished pleasure had far more to do with his deafness than with him. At the start of each journey he would be full of fun, jokes and reminiscences. Any trip down the M4 quickly produced the legendary story of the glorious art-deco Hoover Factory as we passed it, and George's fond recollection that its purpose – in his words to 'suck up shit' – had prompted his employment by Mick Mulligan. But the difficulty of responding in the road noise made any kind of real exchanges impossible. The only way to talk to him was to put an arm around his shoulder and talk quietly into one ear but in his back-seat refuge, complete with battered briefcase and other luggage, this was an impossibility. Seated in the front passenger seat I found that one way was to place George behind the driver, thus making eye, and sometimes verbal, contact possible. But it was generally a losing battle and, soon into the journey, our guest would doze off as usual, waking only to bark 'Where are we?' or to haul himself out for a coffee break at a service station. On one occasion, wandering round in one of these, while wearing his tracksuit bottoms (rechristened appropriately 'heart-attack pants') he fell again while buying sausage and chips. He hauled himself resolutely to his feet and was visibly pleased to find the staff ready and eager to replace his meal for no charge.

'I need some food now we're here,' he announced on arrival at Harewood House in Leeds later in the year. I went in search of the waiter.

'They've only got bar snacks, I'm afraid, George.'

'Bath mats?' responded my friend, deploying his gorgonesque stare.

For the next few months, as his ribs and collarbone recovered, George seldom fell short on-stage. Our show had turned into a smoothly running, fine-tuned presentation, punctuated by jokes which George saw as part of his role. Most of them — to the delight of the crowd, as well as the group — were dirty ones.

For his opening number, George was now resigned to 'Old Rockin' Chair' followed by his celebrated Viagra gag — frequently capped with its F-word punchline. If the laugh was big and unqualified, almost anything could follow:

'There were two dogs at the vet's, and one's looking glum. The other one says, "Why are you here?" And he says, "Well, yesterday my master left me alone in the flat for hours — and I was taken short, wasn't I? I went everywhere; on his bed, on the Afghan carpet, everywhere. So he's brought me here to have me put down." The other one says, "I'm not surprised you're looking glum!" So his new friend says, "Well, why are you here?"

'"Well, last night I saw my mistress in a baby-doll nightdress bending over the oven. And I couldn't resist it, could I? I went and got the old leg over!"

'"So has she sent you here to have you put down?"

'"No! She's brought me here to have me nails trimmed!"'

George, of course, loved his home town of Liverpool, and this became a theme for another favourite.

'People sometimes ask me, "Why haven't you got a Liverpool accent?" "Well, I haven't, but I can do one and I'll tell you a joke to prove it." [He relapses into authentic Scouse.]

'A bloke comes home and finds his wife in tears. "Wharra marra then?"

'"It's the kids! They never stop swurring! Swurr, swurr, swurr – that's all they ever do!"

'So the man says, "I can see you're oopset! Well, you stay in bed in the morning and I'll bring you oop a nice cuppa tea. And then I'll go down and I'll sort 'em out."

'So next morning he goes down to find the two boys – one nine, one eleven – and he says to the eldest one, "Wharra yer want for your breakfast, son?" And th' boy says, "I'll 'ave a fuckin' egg!" Bang, crash [this part of the narrative illustrated with spirited swipes at the air], leaves him snivelling in a corner. So then he says to the younger son, "And what do you want for your breakfast, son?' And the younger boy says, "Well, I won' 'ave a fuckin' egg for a start."'

Quite the rudest one was usually saved for the show's end when all the ice was not only broken but in a state of total meltdown.

'I live in Shepherd's Bush. They have a market there which sells RUBBISH in general. And one day while I was there I saw two ladies coming out of a flower stall. And one says to the other (this in perfect Max Miller cockney):

'"Isn't that your old man coming out of that flower stall?"

'"Yes, and 'e's got two dozen roses – blast it!"

"'Why 'blast it'?"

"'Well, it means I've got to spend the 'ole of the weekend on me back with me legs in the air." [A long pause.]

"'Oh . . . why don't you buy a vase?'"

Very few people complained to us about such ribaldry; in fact only one person ever did. A dignified lady in Blackpool made her displeasure felt to me but what could one say? 'If you come to see George Melly,' I tried to explain, 'you come to see George Melly.' Possibly any sense of outrage was defused because the Half-Dozen were sturdy and ever-enthusiastic straight men and made a point of laughing themselves silly on-stage, even if they'd heard the joke several dozen times before. This was a contrast to the Feetwarmers who, at least later on, tended to present an on-stage image of reserve, leaving the laughter to the audience. But occasionally, and perhaps a little wickedly, in a form of showbusiness hara-kiri, George would call our collective bluff.

'You've heard it before, you know!'

'It's the way you tell 'em' was our only available response. But what was flattering and good to hear from audiences was that they liked the way we supported George on-stage. 'You really do look after him,' supporters were often heard to say. And, beyond pleasure, the only possible response was, 'We wouldn't be here without him!'

Only twice did I feel an (unjustified) twitch of reserve. Perhaps on a concert in Derry, it may have been a risky place to tell this one:

'An Englishman, a Scotsman and an Irishman were discussing their preferred watering holes. And the Englishman said, "Well, near where I live in Guildford [George's jokes were often tinted with small focused details] I know a pub where between 6 and 7 you actually get all your beer for half price. They call it the Happy Hour." And the Scotsman looks scornful and says,

"Aye, that's nothing. I know a tavern in Glasgow where if you buy a pint of ale you get a wee-heavy whisky for nothing!" And the Irishman says, "That's nothing. I know a place where you get all your drink free – all night – and at the end of the night you get laid too!" So the Englishman and Scotsman look at him in amazement and say, "Have you been there? Where is it?" And the Irishman says, "Well, I've not been there meself – but me sister has!"'

George's mindshifts occasionally lent his jokes a surreal turn. Strangely enough, as a practised drinker myself, I could often identify the moment when he might slip or (very occasionally) fluff a punchline producing what Julian aptly called 'the Tumbleweed effect' – bewildered silence from the audience. But one day he had me fooled. We were playing in Birmingham in a beautiful open-air square in front of a handsome church, and our journey to the Second City had recalled the ribald tale of a fellow musician, known to us all, and his Black Country girlfriend. He had picked her up from work and asked if she'd like a coffee.

'Naow, luv! Can we go 'ome right away? I've bin feelin' foonye all day.'

So home they went to go straight to bed. And afterwards our friend had asked if everything was all right.

'Foine!' said his friend. 'I've coom twice actuallie!'

This story tickled George immensely and the punchline stayed in his mind. So that when he arrived on-stage, facing not only a capacity crowd but the vicar of the handsome building to his rear as well as his wife and several sub-teenage children, he looked absently down, announced to his audience 'I've coom twice actuallie!' and burst into roars of laughter. While the gentleman of the cloth and his family stared back mystified – and presumably mortified too.

For the remainder of 2004 we carried on working steadily: at the beautiful Court Theatre in Tring; back to Cole Mathieson's Concorde Club in Eastleigh, Epsom Playhouse, the magnificent Reading Concert Halls, Telford, Chelmsford and Barrow-in-Furness. Years before, George's outdoor knee-tremble after a gig in Barrow with Mick Mulligan's band had been unexpectedly illuminated for all to see by the eruption of a nearby blast furnace. 'I could see old Fat's arse,' reported drummer Pete Appleby, similarly engaged at the time, 'going up and down like the clappers!'

It was early in April that year, though, that I had my first small disagreement with George. We had gone to play two nights at the Plough Arts Centre, Torrington, in Devon, a small but exquisite venue with hosts nearby who lived in an ancient, but magnificently restored, antique manor house, complete with wooden pews around a roaring open fire, mulled wine and bedrooms hidden above the winding turret stairs of an east and west wing.

But the row began after the second show when, tired and loaded with vodka, I was busy dismantling George's stall, repacking his books and CDs and wrestling with the recurring troublesome questions of commission to the venue and VAT invoices. I had promised to bring George his favourite Irish whiskey but had forgotten in all the business. Over came our star.

'You said five minutes!' he hissed, pointing ostentatiously to his watch. 'And now it's exactly seventeen!'

'I'll be with you,' I said briefly; I bought the whiskey and handed it to him. 'Perhaps next time you'll remember that it's me – not you – that arranges your sales, packs your books and makes all the money while you take it easy. I really don't see why you can't buy your own.' And I walked off in a huff.

This would not be our first disagreement over the next year or so. I began to realise more vividly that working for George did not just entail playing for – or with – him. You were often hired help. And slowly – just as it may have done for John Chilton – the worm of jealousy began to stir within me. I had led the band, written the arrangements and provided George with a new musical context which was plainly working, and an album which he quickly described as his 'best ever'. And yet here I was, carting boxes of books, folding trestle tables and acting visibly to our departing audience, not as a high-profile bandleader who'd just left the stand, but as an off-stage serf. I tried to resist the feelings. And next morning, as the vodka and ire had cooled off simultaneously, I was as quick to apologise to him as he was to me.

We continued our busy round, regularly three or four concerts in a row, in Northampton, Pinner, Sevenoaks, Hungerford, lovely Horsham, Leek in Staffordshire, four nights at the Maidstone Pizza Express, East Kilbride, Carlton in Bedfordshire at John Tusting's wonderful barn theatre ('Let's do the show right here!'), Leeds, Stockton-on-Tees, Winchfield, Blackpool, Royal Tunbridge Wells, at the legendary Bull's Head for Dan Fleming in Barnes; all these had us referring to our battered atlases until July. But soon a new unforeseen hazard was to assail us. It would become immortalised to the Half-Dozen as 'the Watfords'.

CHAPTER EIGHT

Blues for Watford Gap

In late July 2004 we were due to take to the road again, this time for Altringham, then on to Bury for two days at their Arts Centre. Altringham, as usual, was a sell-out and our comfortable hotel a pleasure. Next morning Lisa, as ever my faithful driver and tireless helper, had checked out with me and together we were awaiting George in the hotel car park. There he was, making his dignified walk towards the car, candy-cane suit unmistakeable in the morning sun. But, as he opened the door, he turned back.

'I won't be long,' he said.

But he was gone some time and after a while I crossed the car park to chat with Julian and Craig waiting, in their own vehicle at the roadside, the departure of our convoy to Bury.

'I don't know where he's gone,' I said at last.

'There he is,' said Julian.

And indeed it was George who appeared, as he remade his way across the long parking area, to have swapped his suit trousers for a natty pair of shorts, scarcely visible beneath his jacket.

'I've never seen him wear those before,' I said.

'Wear what?' said Julian. 'I don't want to worry you, Dig. But I don't think he's wearing anything at all.'

As George got closer, it was clear that Julian was right. Our star was naked from the waist down and as I walked back to Lisa's car he greeted the two of us jovially.

'Had a bit of an accident,' he said. 'Haven't shat myself in some time now. But I've had to dump most of my stuff in the hotel gents. IMPOSSIBLE [George still frequently talked in capitals] to get to the room in time.'

This was awkward. The clean-up operation had not been entirely successful and tell-tale hints, both visual and sensory, lent vivid witness to the problem as George settled himself, as nature intended, into the back seat and our bizarre convoy began its journey.

On arrival in Bury it was necessary to get George – semi-naked but gloriously unconcerned – into our guesthouse and cleaned up. I was perturbed; this was a new threat to us, though tales of George's incontinence had echoed around the jazz scene for several years. One fan, back in the Feetwarmers days, had visited the men's room only to find the star of the show chatting happily as he washed his underpants out in the basin.

Lisa as ever was a tower of strength. Together we went shopping for new tracksuit trousers, towels and underwear, a crusade which took up most of the afternoon. Once the trip was complete, there was just time to re-equip our star, make for the theatre for a sound check and then hurry back for an all-too-brief sojourn in our accommodation before heading back to the theatre again for the show proper.

George, delightfully, wasn't worried at all, but I was. The problem – compounded by a day without my usual siesta – meant that I hit the stage rather too full of vodka for comfort and by the end of the night – after a show featuring a similarly inebriated George – I was both drunk and furious. A spat with drummer Bobby Worth fuelled my rage and – despite Lisa's wise advice to 'let it go' – I galloped down the stairs to confront my star.

'Damn it all, I've had enough. First you cover our car in shit. Then you get drunk! The show was bloody awful. Really I don't know what the fuck you think you're doing! Frankly, I've fucking well had enough.'

George – to his credit – seldom lost his temper as I did that night and his responses were blurred but measured and conciliatory. But I couldn't be comforted or pacified and slammed up to my room in a huff. 'That's it,' I said to Lisa, who knew that when drunk I had a temper. As usual, she absorbed my anger with philosophic resignation, knowing that, come the morning, anger would have given way to alcoholic remorse.

Which of course it did. By the journey home, George and I had become the best of friends again. But the gloves had come off and might well do so again: our honeymoon period had come to an end. I also began to understand why John Chilton had passed through his own 'drinking days' at one earlier point in his career. It was obvious that driving Mr Melly, as well as being his bandleader, produced its share of unscheduled complications as well as the ones I was getting used to.

And John Chilton, so said George, had had temper tantrums too. On one occasion, after a sell-out concert at the Red Lion, Hatfield, the Feetwarmers had been refused a drink. 'Oh,' said John, 'no drink, eh? Well, then, you won't be needing these, will you?' And with a grand sweep of his arm he had sent a barful of empty glasses crashing to the floor. Later on in his career John drank nothing stronger than tea.

The big problem we faced now was that members of the Half-Dozen were less than willing to drive George to and from his concerts. Plainly the band fee of £50 was no longer enough for the new risks involved. Once again Lisa came to the rescue. She had had to have her car valeted following the Altringham altercation and contacted Diana Melly with whom she was good friends. An arrangement was made. From now on any driver who transported George would be paid a full £150 plus a proportion of his petrol costs. This was a huge improvement and much reduced the tension with which I had to face the business of delegating the driving chores. Including our concert fee (usually around £160), a member of the Half-Dozen could make over £300 for a night's work, provided he was prepared to take the gamble of a Melly-induced back-seat crisis. And although a few members continued to abstain from offering their vehicles as transport facilities, Julian, Dominic, Craig, and later Nick Millward, remained happy and hospitable auto-hosts to their venerable guest.

The actual crises thereafter were comparatively few, though in the months to come several members of the Half-Dozen answered the imperious call from the back seat requesting, 'We have to stop – now!' On a busy motorway where actually pulling over to stop was illegal, this could present problems, but on at least one occasion Craig was forced to the roadside while his passenger lowered everything below the waist at maximum speed to the bemused preoccupation of drivers passing at a similar rate. When George had to go, he had to go – and fast. On another occasion in Worcester – at less than five minutes to our destination in the middle of the busy town centre – Dominic and I were forced to plant ourselves at pavement-side while George, squatting on his seat with an open back door, turned ninety degrees to pee prolifically into another rolling river of shoppers engaged in Saturday-afternoon retail therapy. At one point, when such crises had come to a temporary halt, the Melly management proposed that our supplementary pay-ment be confined to occasions on which emergency evacuations actually took place but – after much thought – I decided to remain firm, on the clear-and-present-danger principle.

And what were we to call this increased wage? A week or so after its negotiation Lisa and I drove passed Watford Gap and – aficionados of rhyming slang that we were – the new rate would for ever after be known as 'the Watford' allowance.

After Altringham and Bury, it was perhaps lucky that we had a month to refocus our thoughts, negotiate the Watford agreement and take things (a little) easier. For the first time since our first concert two years previously, work looked like steadying up a little. Nonetheless, as summer moved into autumn, we played both the Exeter Jazz Festival and luxurious Waddesdon Festival on the Rothschild Estate where every musician was given a beautiful ornamental clock (in addition to a handsome fee) and where, in compensation, a large brandy and a beer cost £12.

Meantime, I was still busy and working again with the Pizza All Stars, and on occasion, George Webb's legendary Dixielanders. Following a visit to the Guernsey Jazz Festival for good friend Trevor Cleveland, I toured the Channel Islands – Sark, Alderney and Jersey – with Craig Milverton and a new friend, bassist Bill Coleman, who doubled his brilliant bass playing with a long career as special-material writer for nationally known comedians and a long sojourn with the brilliant comedy rock group the Barron Knights. Bill's routines were as funny as his bass playing was superb and he could easily be left on-stage to keep people amused for hours.

'A man's walking through the Pigalle in Paris late one night and a soft feminine voice whispers, "Excuse-moi, monsieur. How would you like soixante-neuf?"

'"So what am I going to do with five dozen eggs at this time of night?"'

By October we were busy again: Jack Higgins's marvellous *Giants of Jazz* show was back on the road, visiting both the tiny Swan Theatre in High Wycombe and the magnificent Lowry

Theatre in Salford and back to Royal Tunbridge Wells. Now that George knew he no longer had cancer he was back to his normal exhuberant form. Our journeys – now fortified with protective blankets, cushions and a select supply of sanitary underwear – remained hilarious (and untarnished by nature).

At the end of November 2004 we returned to a packed Norwich Playhouse, then flew to Aberdeen, Edinburgh and Glasgow for a three-night tour of Scotland with Chris Barber's band. It was on this trip that I got to know Chris: a master of bandleading who gave me useful tips about our presentation ('Some of the numbers a bit long perhaps?') and taught me an invaluable bit of domestic knowhow – always put the milk in after the boiling water has hit the teabag.

Then, following a charming trip to the tiny St Donat's Arts Centre in Wales, it was time to buckle our belts for our second sell-out Ronnie's season – Monday, 13 December through to New Year's Day with just three days off to be with family and friends – Christmas Eve, Christmas Day and Boxing Day. This time Craig and I stayed at the empty flat of a north London friend, Daphne Shoolman, ate well every day and spent most of the rest of the daylight hours reading, relaxing or just sleeping. For the second year, Ronnie's was having its way with us. And top of the bill with Ray Gelato's Giants in roaring support we were – in that good old jazz phrase – having ourselves a ball.

CHAPTER NINE

On the Road and Radio

As 2005 got into its stride, work with George continued to level out, but we still plied our wares regularly, and during winter and early spring played Cambridge, Dublin's magnificent concert hall (where we outsold every previous visiting jazz act, including the three Bs, Chris Barber, Kenny Ball and Acker Bilk), Uckfield, Loughborough, Chelmsford, the Marlowe Theatre, Canterbury, for a return visit with the *Giants of Jazz* package, plus four nights at the Pizza on the Park (now renamed 'Larry's Room' in memory of the late Larry Adler, a regular habitué), where drummer Nick Millward joined the band permanently.

We also played for the first time at a new club called The Sands in Gainsborough. North of Lincoln, east of Rotherham, Gainsborough is something of a ghost town, its central position as a producer of armaments in the Second World War commemorated only by the shells of once-bustling munitions factories and a modern town centre which seems unsure of why it is there.

Gainsborough, however, is a base for the flourishing Wilkinson's multi-purpose cut-price chain stores, now more than 75 years old. We had a Wilkinson's in Southend and I often shopped there. But Gainsborough, on the face of it, seemed an unlikely location for any sort of British 'jazz corner of the world'. Surprise, surprise, however. One of Wilkinson's directors, Peter Swann, had bought the old town hall and converted it to a state-of-the-art jazz club. A lavish oak-lined entrance hall led to stairs (lined with mega-portraits of British stars from John Dankworth and Cleo Laine to George himself) up to the first floor where a luxurious dining-room faced a dance floor and stage equipped with the most up-to-date amplification, widescreen television and full video recording facilities streamed to the Internet. Peter had already signed bandleader Pete Long to an in-house position as musical director and masterminded a Rat Pack package, whose Sinatra he had recorded with Pete's orchestra for an album and video at London's legendary Abbey Road. And currently he was in negotiation to set up a string of performing centres in China; hits on the Internet from China (apparently a high-interest area) for live shows from The Sands would then be toured at a chain of major stadium venues throughout the country. This was big news.

George was delighted with his portrait and even more with The Sands VIP lounge, set aside for visiting musicians and local dignitaries. Luxury leather suites nestling in thick carpeting faced a bar offering free drinks, coffee and gourmet food; in short – as one rueful sideman observed – the 'kind of conditions we always thought we should be accustomed to'. George attracted a healthier crowd than many of the visiting jazz shows (it was in fact difficult for Jack Higgins to staff their initial seven-day-a-week jazz policy with sufficient acts) and he and I returned there at the end of May for a JazzAid concert, where we appeared alongside Sir John Dankworth and Dame Cleo Laine, Jacqui Dankworth, Tina May, the dynamic young trombonist Dennis Rollins, Courtney Pine and Pete Long's all-star orchestra.

Thanks to Jack Higgins once again, I had joined forces with George as his writer for a Radio 2 series commissioned by David Roper's Heavy Entertainment company, and to be called *It's Trad, Dad*. The title wasn't encouraging but the subject was: a history of revivalist jazz in Britain from its beginnings to the present, including interviews with key figures, recorded music and of course George as presenter, using scripts to be written by me.

This shouldn't have been a problem but George, as a centre-piece of the movement, approached his collaborator's scripts with understandable caution. After all, he had been there and lived through the glory days of the revival when, as he said, 'walking down Oxford Street was equivalent to walking through Storyville'. He had known the inside stories of the passions, the laughter, the frustrations and had heard the sibling amateur music of British believers as they bought their instruments, learned to play 'on the job' and recognised the great voices of classic American jazz as they grew to maturity. I, on the other hand, had learned of those days through books, not at first hand, and was therefore liable to reproduce the half-truths that once prompted Henry Ford to dismiss most of history as bunk.

I knew the problems, as well as the qualifications, that George must have had; the same as those that my old friend the veteran double-bass player Tiny Winters had experienced when he complained of 'younger generations trying to rewrite our history for us'. But, so I thought, with collaboration and careful work from me, we should get through. And after all, what was this? A short radio series – interesting enough to be sure – but very unlikely to find its way into any kind of bibliographic history.

I hadn't reckoned on George's determination, however. My attempt at an initial draft script arrived back covered in scrawled corrections, adjustments and redefinitions. It looked as if the whole thing would have to be written again. But George's comments had also redefined the shape of the whole series, which would certainly not please our producer. This was a problem.

George's point – amplified considerably – was that there was a difference between revivalist jazz (which based itself loosely on the classic recordings of Armstrong, King Oliver and Jelly Roll Morton) and New Orleans revivalism as personified by Ken Colyer. I took his point completely (perhaps the matter had been understated?) and adjusted the script accordingly, but back it came again. I looked at the fee, counted the hours of work involved in constant rewrites, and decided that it might be better if George wrote the series himself. I mentioned the idea to Jack Higgins.

'You fuckers!' yelled my agent and mentor. 'I'm fucking sick of the both of you. All this time I spend in getting you this work and all you do is fuck around with me. Call yourselves professionals? Fuck the pair of you!' Down went the phone.

This was now an awkward matter and I rang the producer to explain the problem. 'Don't worry,' he said comfortingly. 'George always does this. Just get on with it and everything will be fine.'

It probably would have been but on our third night at Larry's Room both the star and his bandleader were, in jazz terminology, 'feeling no pain'. Driving back in Craig Milverton's car with George talking loudly to Lisa, I heard a word I didn't like.

'Your man,' accused George, 'knows nothing about the subject! He wasn't there. And consequently he's nothing less than a LIAR!'

I flared and shot across the back seat in dangerous risk of grabbing my fellow passenger's lapels. 'Don't you ever accuse me of lying,' I screamed, 'and especially not to my partner! Fuck you! I know a lot about this music you seem to think you own. And, apart from the fact that I'm a musician and you're not, I've spent a lifetime in the music too. So don't condescend to me, you fat bastard! And apologise now! To Lisa and to me.'

'Dig,' said Craig, looking alarmed. 'Take it easy. He's drunk. Take no notice!'

'Maybe he is,' I said dangerously. 'But he'd better shut it now or we'll be out of this car together.'

It was the usual drunken shout-up. But plainly the strain of our relationship was starting to tell and, as bandleader and star were both drinking quite heavily, flashpoints were liable to occur. As usual, though, with sobriety came reconciliation. And we were still busy.

As spring began to bloom we played Burgess Hill, Sir John Dankworth's glorious Stables Theatre at Wavendon, back to Barrow-in-Furness for the third time, Littlehampton at the new Windmill Entertainments Centre, and even Warner's Hotel at Hungerford, where peacocks strutted in the grounds and a packed crowd had gathered for a jazz weekend, co-starring Sir John, Dame Cleo Laine and Bill Ashton's wonderful National Youth Jazz Orchestra.

We played Belfast too, and it was here that George once again evinced his talent for making friends where and whenever. The Half-Dozen had gone in search of a pub and received a sobering warning. 'There is a pub round the corner,' said an adviser. 'But don't go in. It's got a violent reputation and only a day or two ago a man was beaten up and killed in there. There's another one fifteen minutes away. Go there.'

We took the hint. But after the performance George's detective qualities went to work. 'Nonsense,' he boomed. 'There's a perfectly good pub just around the corner.'

'George,' protested Dominic. 'It's really dangerous – a no-go area.'

But already our star was on his merry way and cautiously,

after a band conference, we followed George in to discover him surrounded by fans and genially holding court.

It was soon after this that George and the Half-Dozen played Goring Jazz Club, a village hall, packed to the rafters with seats spread over the stage and hall in tight-knit ranks and standing room only in the foyer. The Half-Dozen and its star guest were crowded on to a tiny makeshift podium a matter of inches from the inquisitive faces of front-row guests. And in the dressing room – equipped with a table piled liberally with hospitality from our hosts – it seemed likely that every fire regulation set up by Goring District Council was being comprehensively overlooked.

It's lucky we're near the river, I thought.

Our show proceeded with its customary panache and at half-time Julian and I manned the stall, loaded as usual with CDs and books and handily set up on a canteen-counter leading to the foyer. The queue stretched a long way and after the show we returned to our salesmen's duties only to be interrupted by a worried-looking guest.

'I think,' he said, 'that you ought to come and see Mr Melly.'

Julian and I hurried back-stage to find our star peacefully asleep on the dressing-room floor. Nearby were an empty bottle of Jameson's whiskey (his favourite) and one of red wine, and George had drunk the lot.

Heroically, Julian and I lifted our guest to the back of the car and began the journey home accompanied by a surreal if subtone monologue from our passenger in which, as we neared west London, only the word 'piss' was audible. Julian pulled hurriedly to the side of the road and we hoisted him up against a tree while the call of nature was generously answered by our star. Then, after arriving at George's house, we helped him up one flight of stairs (several falls but no submissions) and into a deep and comfortable armchair in his sitting-room from which he waved us a beatific but silent goodnight.

Diana found him there next morning and was far from pleased. On the following Monday – unlucky 13 June – it was time to record our (now resolved) *It's Trad, Dad* series, on which the presenter's delivery was noticeably more plummy and luxurious than usual. But next day the news came: our two concerts that week, at Nottingham and the Ashcroft Theatre, Croydon, were summarily cancelled. 'It's bronchitis!' yelled Jack down the phone. 'Nothing more.' And sure enough, by Sunday, after (presumably) an intensive course of 'rehab', our star was ready to fly with us to Glasgow Jazz Festival. Then the following week, back on the road we went. Two nights in Havant followed by another at Tunbridge Wells's E.M. Forster Theatre and, last of all, an early-evening show at the remarkable Redoubt Fortress in Eastbourne: a venerable and impressive naval defence stoutly separated from the tides by high walls and boasting a sound system to die for. I had never heard my friend (dressed in a fetching multi-coloured kaftan) sing more strongly and after our show even he was prepared to agree, despite an inbuilt and sedulous capacity for self-critique. It had been a fabulous concert.

CHAPTER TEN

Back in the Groove

Now, the summer of 2005, it was time to consider the matter of a second album for George. At 1.00 a.m. the phone rang again and it was Jack Higgins. 'I have a surprise for you! You've got a new album deal – with Candid. Sort out a budget and let me have it. Right away.'

This was a surprise indeed. Candid remains a high-profile label, founded in America and later taken over by my good friend Alan Bates, formerly the mastermind behind Black Lion Records, the recording home for British traditionalists. For Alan's old company I'd recorded my first solo albums. I'd also worked for a year or so around 1977 at his Hammersmith office, as a producer and all-round helping hand, as a buffer against the threat of full-time work in jazz pure and simple. Since then we'd stayed in friendly and regular touch. During the 1980s he'd both produced my *Portrait* CD compilation and later signed the Great British Jazz Band for three successful albums.

But the offer, however welcome, put me in a quandary. Peter Clayton, the producer of our first album with George as well as my own second band album, *Things Ain't What They Used To Be*, had become a firm friend by now, and had remained in constant touch, the offer of a second album with George being very much on the table. The problem was that Jack Higgins and Peter had had trouble getting on. Peter found Jack frosty, hard to talk to and impatient. Jack, in turn, complained that sales figures and related business returns were slow in coming in. And George, for no reason that I could see, had decided that the 'sticker' issue surrounding his much-prized quote from Sir Paul McCartney had branded Peter an amateur.

There didn't seem to be much I could do. I had to tell Peter and I knew that he was upset and hurt, though he put a brave and cheerful face on the matter. I couldn't blame him and neither could bassist Len Skeat, one of my oldest friends on the scene. 'Come on, Dig,' he insisted. 'Own up! We all know it's very unfair . . .' Which in a way it was. But caught between two friends and professional colleagues I could either face the dismissive wrath of Jack by arguing the case or go with a mechanism set up by the agent, who for thirty years had directed both George's, and latterly my, career. As well as the fate of the Half-Dozen. It seemed there could be no choice.

Soon after this predicament was temporarily resolved, for better or worse. Perhaps it was lucky that George Melly and the Digby Fairweather Quartet (Craig Milverton, Len Skeat and Bobby Worth plus their distracted leader) were offered the respite of a cruise around the Norwegian fjords during the month of August. Beyond the chance of a holiday I wasn't over-excited by the project. Based on my O Level Geography (failed) I had presumed that the fjords would simply constitute a set of navigable impasses surrounded by some sort of green flatlands. But of course I was wrong. Opening our cabin curtains in early August 2005, we saw stone-blue mountains rising to snowy peaks, flecked with tiny technicolour dwellings and between them slim white waterfalls gushing from the mountain heights to the waters beneath us. Green flatlands too, but dotted with enchanting homesteads as sweetly pretty as Swiss cuckoo clocks. As he saw these overpowering beauties for the first time, Bobby Worth, back with the quartet as a regular with the band, broke into tears of joy.

We were in for a relaxed time of it too. Our kindly hostess, the classical impresario Kim Colwell, had indeed scheduled us an easy run for our money and we were to play just two concerts with George throughout the week. Then, beyond a dual-header *Desert Island Discs* show hosted by the enchanting Kim, we were free to wander the decks, explore local haunts in dock and tone ourselves up in the ship's fitness suite and pool. Our hostess carried a packed case of classical CDs and high-quality player with her. And an enduring memory is of Len Skeat listening as the music of Mahler in her headphones magnified the monumental might of the scenery around him. 'It makes us all seem so small,' said my friend, his eyes brightened with a glint of joy.

In fact we were due to play so little that – after a night or two – creative musical juices began to flow and someone suggested a late-night jam session in the ship's main lounge. Why not? Good idea! So, each evening thereafter we took to a corner of the lounge to play for a shipful of people from grandmothers to toddlers for whom the sea breezes had apparently produced an appetite for swing.

All this went well and on the last night our star guest was happy to join us. A thrill of expectancy filled the room as he made his airy entrance, glorious in an exotic kaftan with buttons at the neck, and took his seat to sing the blues and other of his specialities. But by the end of the night, however, fuelled with our favourite tipples, the leader and singer had the wind behind them.

'Go on, George! "Shave 'em dry"!'

George leaned forward in his chair, spectacularly baring his chest.

'I've got nipples on my titties . . .' There was a sudden rush as mature ladies of the audience and mothers covering their toddlers' ears raced from the room like lemmings, in all probability, it seemed to me, making for the other side of the ship and comforting protection of the sea.

But back home again it was time to begin planning our new album, this time for Candid Records.

To begin with, I was determined that our new project would be recorded like a pop album – laying down rhythm tracks first, then vocals and adding brass, strings and other extras later, rather than doing it the old way of 'down in one'; everyone in the studio recording at one time. That method was the proud boast of old-time studio players, recording three or four times a day, year in year out in studios, but that was then and this was now; a time when many jazz players didn't see the inside of a studio once in a year. My way would mean no half-hearted takes or, worse, mistakes. It would be good to mix the music in Julian's new state-of-the-art home studio. And new repertoire was popping into my head too. Fun, I thought, to rewrite the weathered music-hall anthem 'Mr Gallagher and Mr Shean' (made famous by Bing Crosby and Johnny Mercer) telling the broad story of George's life. Fun, too, to update 'Gone Fishing' as a duet for us both. And I even had an original up my sleeve, a dance anthem designed for the elderly, which I decided to call 'The Trudge'. George as usual was the perfectly compliant collaborator. 'Not that keen on all those things,' said our accommodating singer. 'But, if you want, I'll do them!'

Another development was that on this album guests were to make an appearance. Jack Higgins was sure that Jacqui Dankworth would be a perfect duettist with our star and together we decided on two titles: 'The Big Butter and Egg Man' and, more predictably perhaps, 'Let's Call the Whole Thing Off'. Then, one evening at his regular venue, the

Chicken Shed Theatre in Enfield, Julian met Tobias Hug. Tobias was a member of the Swingle Singers, the classic group founded by Ward Swingle in the 1960s and now consisting of a bright new young team. 'Yes!' said Toby. 'We'd love to be on the album. And for free if you want!' Marvellous!

Perhaps the most unexpected and spectacular guest to be approached, however, was Van Morrison, by now an international superstar. I'd met him on odd occasions in the late 1970s with his former colleague John Altman but never since. In fact one night when the two of them had come to Pizza Express to see a small group of mine, I'd made the serious misjudgement of announcing his presence to the audience and our celebrated visitor was off and up the stairs like a turkey through the corn. To my delight, however, Van had requested a full set of our *It's Trad, Dad* collaboration from Heavy Entertainment and it was clear that he retained a strong affection for the British heroes of traditional jazz. On one recent album Acker Bilk had made a welcome appearance, and George had been invited to sit in with 'Van the Man' on live appearances at festivals. I couldn't believe that he would do it but, after letters passed between George and his management, the agreement was set. Van Morrison would indeed duet with George for two tracks on the album, and I began friendly dialogue with his helpful manager Bob Johnson who did everything to make things easy, while protecting the privacy of his client. Yes, Van would be happy to record 'Backwater Blues', it was the first Bessie Smith record he had owned. The key of G would be fine. And we would do an up-tempo blues for track two. However, there were a few unshakeable conditions: his client would receive the same billing in the same-size lettering as the remaining guests; names were to appear in alphabetical order on the CD cover; a first-class hotel was to be located and booked (at his expense) before the session, and there would be no other attempt to cash in on his celebrity. Nor would there be any charge!

I was excited by all this; new arrangements and again, once the creative blister was broken, new lyrics too seemed to fall out of my pen. Very quickly the time came to start recording. So backing tracks – piano, guitar, bass and drums – were laid down at Nick Taylor's Porcupine Studio on 12 October and the following Saturday Van would join us to record live. But the day before, while we were getting ready to play at the Theatre Royal, Margate, Bob Johnson called. 'We can't record Van at Porcupine, Dig,' he said. 'We might have to reschedule or maybe find a studio on the south coast somewhere.' I was worried, this was a last-minute flanker.

'But, Bob,' I said, 'that could be difficult at this sort of notice.'

I didn't like to ask why the veto had been applied but found out later that Van's advance guard had driven past Porcupine Studios and found it to be in nothing more than a medium-sized house, far more modest than our superstar collaborator was used to. But in the event, and generously, Bob (and Van) waived their veto an hour or so later. 'Never mind, Dig,' said Bob, 'Van was going to drive up after his show and stay near the studio. But he's agreed to drive up to Porcupine in the morning instead.'

So, on the morning we gathered at Mottingham, a little on the nervous side. Van, we had been told, should be addressed via his manager, never in person. But promptly at 10 a.m. a limousine drew up and Van Morrison, Bob and a selection of staff stepped out and he walked into the studio.

'Hi, Digby!' he said, extending a hand. 'I haven't seen you since 1979.' I couldn't believe it.

After that things went swimmingly. I handed our two singers their words and efficiently Van marked the verses he was to sing alternately with George. Yes, he preferred modest volume in the studio. And why don't we go for a take? Which we did. With our rhythm section – Craig, Dominic, Len and Bobby – firing on all cylinders, Van with headphones in the studio and George behind glass in the engineer's booth similarly equipped, we knocked off both takes within three-quarters of an hour and then, at his expense again, Van took us all for lunch in an elegant nearby restaurant.

The following week, we added George's remaining vocals to the basic tracks; then on the Wednesday in came the Swingle Singers to record a stylish close-harmony version of 'Straighten Up and Fly Right', to which we would add George's vocal part later. Brass and strings were added in the first week of November and, in the third, Julian, as great an engineer as he is a musician, performed production miracles. When I took the album to a prominent mastering studio in north London they could find nothing to add to Julian's faultless work. This really was an album to reckon with. And when George heard the results he could hardly believe the creations that had grown up alongside his original vocal tracks. 'Quite remarkable,' he said, 'and certainly my finest album! Even if the title has a certain ominous ring to it.' Alan Bates had decided that it would be called *The Ultimate Melly*.

By this time two more Melly books had appeared: the first of them George's *Slowing Down*, a chronicle of his diminishing abilities as old age approached. Typically frank, humorous and observant, it was liked by almost everyone, apart from Jack Higgins. 'Fucking good idea to tell 'em all that,' said his acerbic agent, 'that really should stop you getting any more work.' Which, luckily, it did not. Second to appear was Diana Melly's own cry from the heart, *Take a Girl Like Me*. I liked Diana very much (she had always been friendly as well as understandingly generous over the matters of George's incontinence, extra money for hotel rooms on long trips and so on) but I had reservations over her book. It seemed to me to reveal the thoughts of a woman who lived largely outside the aesthetics and rules of the jazz world and consequently appeared confused by the psyche of the jazz performer. I had also noticed on our phone conversations that, once businesss was concluded (almost always satisfactorily and with generosity), she would put the phone down rightaway, and sometimes declared herself too busy to talk for long as other more urgent matters were awaiting her attention. As she had said on our first meeting, life with George was less fun than it had been in the Mick Mulligan days.

Nevertheless her book received fine reviews almost everywhere. She had clearly endured rough times with George, including extended infidelities, but balls had been present in both courts. Undeterred nevertheless, and with a certain triumph, she embarked, with her husband's full and publicly expressed approval, on a series of appearances at literary lunches and festivals, talking about her forty-year marriage to one of Britain's principal cultural icons.

It was also around this time that Warner Brothers had decided to issue George's celebrated pair of albums *Nuts* and its follow-up *Son of Nuts* as a stylish double CD. By now *Nuts* and its offspring had reached the status of a cult classic. But should we sell this new album at our concerts? Lisa fairly and squarely thought not; it seemed unfair to Peter Clayton, our devoted record producer, and now Alan Bates. And, while I was unsure, George himself, with typical generosity, put the block on the idea too. No, we would sell only our new recordings as we travelled the circuit. Warner Brothers would have to take their chances through the retail outlets. That was all.

With *The Ultimate Melly* completed and production on schedule for Christmas, it was time to go back on the road: with the *Giants of Jazz* (Humphrey Lyttelton and Kenny Ball) at the Chichester Festival Theatre late November, and then our annual visit to Norwich Playhouse, where once again we had the kindest reception from a full house, before our Ronnie's season.

This was to be a long one: five whole weeks running from 12 December 2005 right through to 7 January 2006. Quite a haul but once again the 'house full' signs were up every night, despite the *Evening Standard*'s jazz critic's ritual vilification of George and some of our band. Sir Paul McCartney came in to see us early one evening. Craig and I settled into a friend's Hampstead flat, sleeping much of the day and then getting up for the drive into town for our late-night stints. And, once again, Julian heroically doubled Ronnie's with his Christmas show at the Chicken Shed Theatre, always arriving on time. But it was a killing schedule and, once again, played havoc with my body clock. Already George's new book *Slowing Down* had documented my wrathful dealing with a drunken fan the year before at Ronnie's, who persistently annoyed Melly in the lower bar where we relaxed between sets and sold records. Infuriated, and inflamed with vodka, I had confronted the invader, threatening him with four-letter words (faithfully enumerated and reprinted in George's account – an unfortunate addition to my place in written jazz history), plus threats to have him either thrown out or deal with me personally. The intruder left, luckily perhaps for me.

Ronnie's that year was also the scene for one of George's most self-loved ripostes. He was seldom heckled but on this occasion, having announced a tune by Fats Waller, heard an importunate voice raising a cockney query from the back of the club: ''Oo's Fats Waller?'

George's gorgon stare focused in the direction of his inquisitor. ''Oo's Fats Waller?' he retorted incredulously. 'Who are YOU?' This swift and justified response, and its story, appeared in his act regularly thereafter.

But the strain of performing until all hours night after night, week after week, combined with drink, led me on this season to lay into two of my band colleagues for the comparatively minor mistake of sitting in with our warm-up band, Ray Gelato's Giants. This was the only time that happened but I was ashamed and apologies were necessary in the morning. All in all, despite the success of the season, it was a relief to meet with January and the restoration of a daytime schedule temporarily (at least) devoid of baggy eyes, tired embouchures and booze.

CHAPTER ELEVEN

The Madness of King George

'Dig,' Diana had asked on one of her morning telephone calls. 'Can you remember when George was first diagnosed with dementia?'

I couldn't. But sometime over the past year or so, at one of his now-frequent visits to hospitals and doctors, George Melly had indeed been told that he was suffering from a form of the condition called vascular dementia, a progressively debilitating disease which, like Alzheimer's, gradually reduces the mental faculties of its sufferers. The madness of King George was now official.

Our star, however, seemed blissfully unconcerned. Indeed, it seemed to allow him the option of justifying his inability to remember small inconvenient details. He was happy to announce to friends and audiences alike, 'Well, of course, now you know I'm actually mad!' The thespian within our star seemed to allow him to thoroughly enjoy the admission. And only Jack Higgins felt inclined to explode.

'How the hell,' he roared at his client one morning, 'do you expect me to get you work if you're putting it around that you're mad?'

'It doesn't help if you shout at me, Jack,' observed his client of thirty years imperturbably. 'I can't hear you any better.'

Jack had come up the hard way, as we well knew, and hearing that one of his longest associates and top stars was voluntarily declaring himself insane was not a popular move. George's progressive deafness was making things worse too, particularly as, with the help of an old PR colleague, Jackie Gill, Jack was busy setting up strings of radio interviews for the two of us in order to promote *The Ultimate Melly*, which we completed during January. Their relationship rapidly deteriorated and by the year's end these two old colleagues and sparring partners were no longer speaking to each other.

George's legendary sexuality was becoming a thing of the past too. 'When I was your age,' he had said to me previously, 'I had to tie my cock around my waist. But now' – a wonderful phrase, this – 'it's like being unleashed from a demon!' Just occasionally though the demon would make a valiant return. One afternoon a young Australian blues singer, the daughter of an old colleague, had arrived in England and requested an audience with the master. 'So,' said George, 'we had a pleasant enough chat, though a good deal of the time I had very little idea of what she was saying. And then we went upstairs to listen to some Bessie Smith in my bedroom. At that point she undressed and invited me to get into bed with her. I said, "I'm afraid you'll be disappointed," and indeed all I could produce was a length of old bent hose. But then I suggested she might wank herself off which she did, delightfully noisily, and finally I managed to get half-hard and produce a small reluctant jet of moisture. Which seemed to delight her.'

'Have you tried Viagra?' I asked. 'I can get you some if you want.'

But the old master looked tired. 'I might,' he said. 'But no, I don't think I can be bothered . . .'

Work for George Melly and Digby Fairweather's Half-Dozen was definitely beginning to slacken off. Return visits to previously sold-out venues were sparser than I might have expected. But nevertheless, as winter turned to spring, we returned to old haunts including the Concorde Club Eastleigh for Cole Mathieson, Barrow-in-Furness, as well as the Mick Jagger Centre, Dartford, the Gordon Craig Theatre at Stevenage (where Bob Bustance had fixed jazz concerts for over thirty years), Cranleigh in Surrey, the Dartmouth Music Festival and of course the Bull's Head in Barnes, that west London jazz sanctuary, for good friend Dan Fleming. And the Half-Dozen was starting to work slowly but surely as an independent unit too at the Bull's Head, Huntingdon Hall, Worcester and The Sands at Gainsborough. Much as we enjoyed our shows with George it was good to work as a solo act.

In 2005, and again in 2006, Digby Fairweather's Half-Dozen had fairly and squarely landed the Birmingham Jazz Award for top small group of the year. Several of my fellow players – Julian, Len Skeat and in 2006 Dominic Ashworth – had also won individual awards within their instrumental category. These achievements met with indifference from the oh-so-trendy jazz press but we didn't care. Whatever the papers said, or didn't choose to say, we knew that we were good; that our stage presentation was as polished as any of the better-established bands and that we could do more things well than most of our senior bill toppers. But without George it was still hard to find our way as a single act into most top venues. And as Jack Higgins was quick to affirm we needed that star name.

I was still busy enough anyhow with other projects. Though my close friend of over thirty years, trombonist Pete Strange, had died in 2004, his creation, the Great British Jazz band, was still playing odd concerts with Don Lusher as our new lead trombonist. And, despite Don's advancing difficulties with mild dementia, the Best of British Jazz was still playing too. Most of the great originals – Jack Parnell, Lennie Bush and of course Kenny Baker – had either retired or died. But nonetheless we continued to appear at favourite venues with a show which, though less polished than Kenny's great original (or indeed my own Half-Dozen), still managed to be a crowd pleaser.

Meantime, the indefatigable Jack Higgins had devised yet another new presentation. Simply to be called *The Sounds of Jazz*, it was to feature George, the Half-Dozen and Jacqui Dankworth who had duetted with George on *The Ultimate Melly*. Like most of the rest of us, George had fallen for Jacqui immediately. Exquisitely and classically beautiful with a frank open-throated laugh and a face that could relapse with striking suddenness from mirth to something close to introspective pain, she was also, in all of our opinions, Britain's greatest young jazz singer, with a degree in drama from RADA for good measure. We made our debut at the Anvil Theatre, Basingstoke, on 25 May 2006 to a full crowd and Jacqui was marvellous, collaborating with the Half-Dozen's vocal group for a revised version of my blues 'Babe' and touching the audience's hearts with a deeply felt reading of Burke and Van Heusen's 'But Beautiful'. The only problem came at the end of the concert when, after a minimal rehearsal, George and Jacqui were due to reprise their triumphant recorded success with 'Let's Call the Whole Thing Off' before a packed audience.

'You say neither,' Jacqui began, looking at George expectantly. He leaned forward.

'Pardon?'

'And I say neither,' Jacqui finished quickly. 'You say either . . .'

George stared back in silence with a broad smile.

'And I say either,' sang Jacqui, catching the ball again. Which she continued to do until the song came to a premature and mildly hysterical end.

It was probably the pressure of these unavoidable situations that made me less tolerant than I might have been of George's on-stage eccentricities. A regular intake of vodka did nothing to help the situation either. But at this point George and I were heading for a brief period of dissension. He had spotted that I could become bullish after an intake of what I had christened 'Dr Smirnoff's prescription' and had teased me about it for some time, a forefinger teasingly jerked towards my full on-stage glass discreetly hidden behind a microphone-stand. But now, as the dementia slowly began to take hold, he became critical of our show. Why did our drummer Nick Millward play so loudly? And, come to that, the rest of us too? Why were my announcements so long? Why couldn't we play a more traditional style; maybe introduce a tuba or banjo? And our arrangements, now tightly designed with the occasional reference to contemporary styles, bore little resemblance to the revivalist jazz that he had grown up with and which plainly still beat through his heart like an anthem.

It hadn't always been the case. To begin with George had adored the heavy passionate electric blues that Dominic Ashworth could wring from his guitar and I loved it too. But two more traditionally minded members of the rhythm section felt otherwise and had made no secret of their feelings. Ever the fair and gracious arbitrator, Dominic determined to hold an interview with our star away from the conflicting opinions surrounding him.

'George,' he had said on one return journey, 'can I ask you something?'

'Anything!' came the obliging voice, its owner curled up in the back seat and mellow after a sell-out concert.

'Are you OK with the blues – the electric blues we play behind you on "Trouble in Mind"?'

'If I could have it all the time,' returned George, ever the charmer, 'I would.'

But now things were changing and it was beginning to look as if we might have a difficulty. I valued every member of my Half-Dozen deeply and enjoyed introducing them at the beginning of our show before George came on-stage, after which I said not one word. It was also the case that George knew little about them and in fact had to have their names prominently displayed in a list on his music stand after almost four years! Then there was the more serious matter of the music itself. My band, I felt, had given George a new and diverse context which had refocused him in the public eye after the decline of his career with John's Feetwarmers. And, like any bandleader, I was prepared to defend my musicians from outside attacks. So, for the first time in our relationship it seemed possible that George and I might, however unbelievably, stop being friends.

But meantime we continued to pack them in: at the huge Upton Jazz Festival in June and later in July at a tiny concert with a quartet in Cardiff. And it was here that the first really damaging row broke out.

We had travelled down with my quartet – Dominic Ashworth, Len Skeat and Nick Millward – to our hotel and soon after we arrived I had taken a call on the mobile from our promoter. He had been expecting us to arrive earlier and had been, unknown to us, waiting for over an hour, it seemed. 'Where are you? This is no good.' So around Cardiff centre we drove at breakneck speed to our venue, challenging lights and invading bus lanes to find an angry host, who for the moment seemed reluctant to speak to even or look at me, a tiny stage set with an expensively hired grand piano (not required) and generous PA system.

'Don't worry,' I said, trying manfully to calm the waters, 'everything will be fine.' But our sound check against the clock was difficult and in between I also had to meet and calm a television crew who had arrived to interview George, locate and set him up with his interviewer (explaining the deafness problem as we went) and do my best to comfort our still-distressed employer. All this was complicated by the fact that Babs had arrived at the hotel in a bad temper with her small dog ('not allowed in,' said the manager firmly) after driving around Cardiff for ages, unable to find either her man or the venue. By the time everything was sorted there was very little time to do anything but rush back to the hotel to change, locate a none-too-handy half-bottle of vodka and then drive back to the venue devoid of rest or the turn-off time most players enjoy before a concert. Back at the venue I found a packed house and, luckily, a promoter restored to total bonhomie, prompted by what appeared to be a fair intake of alcoholic aid.

Our first set went faultlessly. But there had been no time to set up George's stall and, when we went back after a warm-up number, I waved to him and announced his reappearance for part two. Our star advanced towards the stage then inexplicably took a right turn and disappeared from view completely. This wasn't the first time this had happened and consequently I launched into an ad-lib blues:

Mr Melly he's gone and he might be quite some time . . .
But when he returns I know everything's gonna be just fine!

Indeed Mr Melly was gone for quite some time and when he made his bemused return our blues had lasted for quite some time too. But he took to the stage and our second half went swimmingly enough. As we left, though, the trouble started. I hastened down the club stairs to perform my standard duty of setting up George's sale table to find Babs, a closed suitcase of books and George in a state of alcoholic impasse. I began to unpack the case.

'What was that extraordinary thing you started the second half with?' enquired the one-time band-singer fixing his now-familiar gorgonesque stare firmly upon me.

'Well,' I said, 'you had disappeared after I announced you! And we had to do something to keep the show going. So I made up a blues about how you'd be back soon.'

'Too long,' rapped my inquisitor, 'I wasn't gone for more than a minute. A piss and three shakes were all.'

'No, George,' I said, 'you were gone for nearly ten. Which didn't make it easy for any of us.'

'No, I wasn't. And what are you doing with that case? You look like a Turkish carpet salesman. Let Babs do it. She does it better than you do anyhow.'

'Well, in that case,' I said, putting my face close to his, my temper cracking, 'let her fucking do it. Fuck you, George. And in future don't fuck with me.'

'I've always wondered if it might be fun,' offered George.

But I was past joking and fumed off back to the hotel, realising that if I never saw George Melly again it really wouldn't, for the moment at least, bother me at all. Unusually the feeling persisted in the newly acquired sobriety next morning and for once there were no apologetic phone calls from either side. Whatever gloves had been worn, it seemed that they were now off, for good and all.

But of course we carried on working. And at our next meeting at the Edinburgh Jazz Festival just over a fortnight later I was at pains to make amends and greet my friend as warmly as he regreeted me. 'Shout-ups' had not been unknown in either Mick Mulligan's band or John Chilton's Feetwarmers and where necessary we were capable of exactly the same exercises.

However, George was now quite as capable of exploding as I was. One band member in particular could get under his skin. By pointing out a 'No Smoking' sign on the flight up to Edinburgh, he had incurred a scream of wrath from our star, which was followed by a tongue-lashing administered to an over-officious air hostess who had seen a closed packet of cigarettes on his flight table.

All this was understandable. George was well aware of his failing capacities but preferred to cope with them himself when and wherever he could. 'I know I'm getting old and infirm,' he told his combatant, 'but where I can I like to be independent. I can SEE signs. I can SEE steps. So don't tell me what to do. Just shut up!' But the anger passed again and our Edinburgh concert was moved by director Mike Hart to a bigger venue on the night, so keen were the visitors to catch up with the one-time Dean of Decadence.

Despite the show's success, though, things were not right next morning. After a pleasant breakfast with American visitors, including Matt Domber (the legendary owner of the marvellous Arbors label 'where classic jazz lives on'), clarinettist Kenny Daverne and drummer Butch Miles, I was summoned imperiously into George's presence as he sat on the steps of the hotel having a smoke.

'I'm afraid,' he said, 'that I'm no longer happy with your band. The drums are APPALLINGLY loud! And the arrangements have nothing to do with jazz as I hear it. Remember what Jelly Roll Morton said, "sweet soft, plenty rhythm . . ."?'

I cut in. 'George,' I said firmly, 'I'm sorry you're no longer happy with us. But we've done you good service for four years now. Your albums have had brilliant reviews. I can't change the sound or the line-up of my band. And honestly, if you want me to rewrite all the arrangements, I'm afraid I'm going to have to charge you.'

'Well, I can always pay you,' said George, 'of course.' But he didn't look happy about it.

'Look,' I said searching for a way to calm troubled waters. 'Why don't we talk about this another time? Perhaps we can meet up, make changes in the programme. Cut down the size of the group on some tunes so the music's softer? I'm sure there's plenty of things we can do. So let's not argue.'

Which we didn't any more that morning. On the way back home from Heathrow, George and I sat in the back of our cab, talking peaceably; a rare opportunity for me to put my arm round my old friend and hold an audible conversation about his life, his relationships and his way of thinking now.

'Do you think it's possible,' I asked, 'that it's the feminine in you that makes it easy for you to absorb neuroses or problematic behaviour in others, including your women friends?'

He looked thoughtful. 'That's a good question,' he said. 'And you might well be right.'

But still the troubles and conflicts were not done. On a menacing date – Sunday, 13 August – we travelled to the Brecon Jazz Festival after an appearance at Lord Montague's fiftieth birthday party for the Beaulieu Jazz Festival. Humph, Acker Bilk and their bands had played. And George, Craig and I had occupied a ten-minute spot in between, for which George, resplendent in a scarlet kaftan, shouted the blues over the grounds where, almost fifty years ago, the trads had battled the mods in a well-remembered and indeed historic British jazz riot.

But this was Sunday and after a concert and a long journey George was tired. The journey across the familiar Welsh territory plainly moved him deeply; he had been the first star of the first Brecon Festival 25 years previously and along the way we caught a brief glimpse of the castle which he had once owned and where, years before, he had retired regularly to fish his beloved private trout stream along the River Usk until the currents had become too heavy for him.

'There it is,' he said, untypically reflective, 'see it? Down there at the end of the track. It breaks my heart to think that I might never see it again . . .'

The magnificent Brecon Festival sports two marquees, one of which is capable of holding over 2,000 people, and there we were, ready to play our show to a capacity crowd. I had just finished setting up George's sale table when a steward approached me.

'Mr Melly requires to see you now in his dressing room.'

I feared the worst and wasn't disappointed. Once again, up came the old complaints: why was the band too loud? Why didn't our arrangements sound more like Jelly Roll Morton's? Why should it be me who made the announcements? Why couldn't we get a tuba?'

'George,' I said tiredly, 'let's forget this for now and just do our show!'

But at the sound check, peopled by technical staff, stewards and curious members of the public, George said something over his microphone at a volume that would have done credit to the Rolling Stones that I wasn't, for once, prepared to let go.

'If of course the band can bear to play softly enough, I think I should be able to hear myself all right.'

I marched over to his side. 'George,' I said, furious, 'if you have comments about my players you will convey them to me privately and they'll be discussed in due course!' Star and bandleader left the stage with cross looks, and attempts by George to carry the conversation further were stalled by an angry trumpeter.

But it was obvious that we now had to do something. And over the next week, before our annual appearance at the

beautiful Mill Theatre up the Thames at Sonning Eye, I recon-
structed George Melly's programme. Out went the dynamic
electric blues of 'Trouble in Mind', the shouting excitement of
'Everybody Loves My Baby', once again featuring Dominic
Ashworth's stoking John Schofield-style guitar. And in came
discreet quartets, including a Feetwarmers'-style 'Wining Boy
Blues', a gentle 'Ain't Misbehaving', featuring just George with
Julian's beautifully restrained clarinet; in short, much less of the
band and much more of George. I felt happier with the
changes.

On the following Thursday, 17 August, I was one of many
guests celebrating George's eightieth at a party at the Cork
Street gallery just off Regent Street. Celebrities such as
Jonathan Miller and David Hockney milled around the packed
gallery holding court or waiting to be recognised as did
members of the classic jazz fraternity, including Jim Godbolt
and, wonderfully, Mick Mulligan with wife Tessa. This was the
last time I would see Mick. Charming as always, full of irre-
pressible swearing and enthusiasm for Kenny Baker, Nat
Gonella and the senior trumpet-masters, we shared a long
conversation.

'Would you,' asked Mick, 'and the Half-Dozen like to play
at my eightieth next January?' He had been at Ronnie Scott's
every New Year's Eve and loved our close harmony version of
George Gershwin's 'Liza'.

'Yes, of course,' I said, 'and we won't charge you a sou. It'll
be a privilege.'

But later there was a flutter of activity in the adjacent room.
Mick had passed out and fallen without warning; people ran to
help him up. But it was obvious that he was alarmed and not
sure where he was and soon after Tessa took him home.

On the following Sunday, with the show revised, we arrived
at the Mill Theatre. At sound-check time George declared

himself pleased with our changes: 'That's exactly right. Thank you!'

But, despite his delight, our star was still a loose canon. At the show's opening he was once again nowhere to be seen.

'Where's he gone?' asked Julian.

'Well,' said a helpful steward, 'we saw him go over the bridge to the pub but we haven't seen him since.'

Julian, ever the hero, went in search of our missing bill topper while, once again, with distinct and now disturbing sentiments of *déjà vu*, I launched into what was now a familiar blues.

Mr Melly's been here but now it seems he's gone
But I can tell you folks you won't have to wait too long . . .

But wait we did. And when he did turn up, rather the worse for wear, our show took the odd surrealistic turn ending with an encore of 'Do You Know What It Means To Miss New Orleans' in which more was missing than just memories of the city. The bemused audience took their leave and once again I found my teeth gnashing with frustration.

'George, will you please do me a favour? Stay on the premises when it's time for the show. And, by the way, try not to fuck up the encore. Begin well, finish well, that's the rule. And you know that as well as I do.'

On the way home George told Len Skeat, 'I got a bollocking!'

The situation was rankling and I knew that sooner or later there was liable to be a meeting and probably a reckoning. On 14 September I had offered to clear Diana Melly's merchandise accounts by returning to her all of George's books and CDs and accordingly called at the house. There I was met by Diana and her accountant in an atmosphere that bordered on the funereal.

'George would like to see you,' said Diana, 'upstairs.'

Up I went to find my inquisitor seated in his big armchair. 'Sit down,' he said, 'because I have several things I want to say to you.'

The phrase 'here we go' crossed my mind, but I reminded myself that my friend was a lifelong hero and one-time role-model. I was determined to keep a smile on my face while I sat on a stool designed, I was sure, to have me crouched at a lower level somewhere around the level of his feet.

'Now!' said my interrogator. 'We have things to discuss!'

'Yes,' I said smiling. 'We do. Tell me what you have to say.'

'Well, to begin with,' said George, 'we must begin with a premise. I think you will agree that the reason you are appearing at so many premier venues, with your admittedly excellent band, is because of me?'

'Certainly,' I said. No one could deny that.

'And that consequently your request for money to rewrite arrangements for me sets a precedent hitherto unacknowledged in our professional relationship?'

'Certainly,' I said, 'and well put. But to be honest, George, after all this time I think you might dismiss that as an idle threat, born of very temporary ire.'

'Ah yes,' said George, 'Dr Smirnoff. We all know about him. But there is one area on which we are at odds musically. You enjoy the word "progression". And I HATE it! Now, would you say you are a nervous person by definition?'

'Possibly,' I said, 'but why?'

'Well plainly,' said George, 'you were out of your social depths at my eightieth birthday party, wouldn't you agree?'

I felt my muscles tighten but kept the smile. 'Well, no, not really,' I said. 'Perhaps with the bigger celebrities. But I didn't talk to them – and they probably had no interest in talking to me.' I was determined not to let that smile break.

'And by the way,' said George, now well into his stride, 'did you know that whenever you ARE that nervous you have the most appalling bad breath?'

This definitely came from left-field! 'No,' I said, 'to be honest I've never connected one with the other.'

'Well, you should,' said George imperiously. 'And I think we must lay down some ground rules from here on. Your drummer will use brushes. Your band will remember that it is accompanying *me*. And I in turn will give full credit to your band members as we go along, thus saving you the trouble.'

My smile had not broken and I took his hand. 'Very well, old friend,' I said. 'Whatever you say is fine with me. And, by the way, I love you!'

'I love you too!' said George and I kissed the top of his head.

As I got downstairs the atmosphere was still muted. I felt like a schoolboy returning to class after a caning, but smiled brightly. 'Everything's fine, Di,' I said, 'and also sorted out. He's a wonderful man. And we have a lot of great things left to do.' She nodded compliantly as I left the house and wandered down the sunlit midday, towards Shepherd's Bush.

Over the coming months, we had a lot to do indeed. A string of Jack's *The Sounds of Jazz* shows with George and Jacqui Dankworth to start with; for millionaire Leon Morelli's Jazz Party at St Austell, at Solihull Arts Complex and the massive North Finchley Arts Department. With George alone and the Half-Dozen we played the posh RAC Club in Pall Mall, the Riverside Theatre Woodbridge, Granville's Restaurant in Stone near Stoke-on-Trent, the Pizza Express at Maidstone (for a two-night season) and even at a brand-new club called Bar Lambs in Station Road, Westcliff, as well as our regular return to the Bull's Head, Barnes.

All these jobs were free of troubles or confrontation. I had determined that there would be no more strife with George; his developing illnesses (now officially diagnosed as vascular dementia as well as a recurrence of the lung cancer he thought he had escaped) were its cause, and our partnership, as well as our friendship, were both too valuable to me to be put at risk.

One place we didn't get back to at the close of 2006 was Ronnie Scott's, at least for our heavyweight season. This, for me, was a relief; the traumas and disagreements of the year previously had made me wary of the risks of weeks of night work and I wanted no more disagreements with my friends in the Half-Dozen.

However, when George found out, he was angry at the discontinuance after 33 years and at one point had threatened to refuse the offer of just three days in November and to transfer his services to the Pizza on the Park, over in west Knightsbridge, for a six-week season. An excellent idea except that, quite possibly to the loss of the management, he hadn't been invited to appear there. But in late November, anyhow, we played three nights back at Ronnie's for Leo Green; the houses were full, conditions and money far superior to previous years, and honour seemed as good as satisfied. It was good to spend Christmas at home and to see the New Year in listening and dancing to Lisa's function band rather than looking out from a crowded stand to the celebrants beyond.

CHAPTER TWELVE

Slowing Down for Sure

The year 2007 started sadly nevertheless. Just before Christmas Mick Mulligan had died from a stroke (from which he never recovered consciousness) and his funeral, organised by a close friend, trumpeter Bill Harvey, was to be on Thursday, 4 January at the Thomas a' Beckett Church in Pagham. Bill had kindly invited me to help play farewell to this grand figure and seminal raver of British jazz. I reached the church in time to see widow Tessa, her daughters, a packed congregation and pews set aside to accommodate a big group of musicians including Bill, trumpeter Cuff Billett, Paul Sealey, Ian Christie, John Barnes, George Walker and more.

George Melly, was there too of course, and had been asked to deliver the eulogy. Carefully avoiding the F word – by spelling it out instead – he made his way through a long and affectionate address which, among other areas, dealt with Mick's first meeting with George Melly Senior.

'My father,' said George, 'said that my mother's coffee tasted like "ferret's piss". Which turned into friends immediately.'

At the back of the church the Minister's good-humoured face failed to blanche for even one second. 'But,' said Roger

Horton, long-time manager of London's 'Home of Traditional Jazz' the 100 Club, later at the wake, 'I doubt if he'd heard those words in church before.'

I felt deeply for George at his loss. He had cried all day at hearing the news and rung Wally Fawkes. 'Well,' said wise Wally, 'there goes our youth.' George had loved that brief epitaph and thereafter quoted it often. But it occurred to me that losing someone as close as Mick might make him secretly wonder if it wasn't getting on for his time to leave.

Then on 10 January the phone rang, and it was Jack.

'I think GM is losing it,' he said. 'You'd better ring Diana then call me back.'

But Diana seemed calm enough. She explained that she'd had a row, had been in tears, but was now fine and walking the dogs.

'How is George?' I asked.

'Well, he's mad now, of course,' she said casually. 'But probably once he's on-stage he'll be just like he always is.'

On a late rainy afternoon soon after, I travelled back home by train from a successful but boozy lunchtime fundraiser concert for the National Jazz Archive at 100 Oxford Street. It had been full enough with a long queue: the star guest was the great Kenny Ball, along with singer Val Wiseman and a distinguished band of mine, assembled by telephone, including Julian, my old friend John Altman (just back from a successful US career as a film composer), Campbell Burnap, John China, Paul Sealey, Pete Skivington and drummer Pete Cater. In the audience was Britain's founder-jazz revivalist George Webb, who donated six of his newest CDs (auctioned for £180) as well as John Chilton, Ron Bowden and Archive stalwarts Stan and Jean Ball, Jayne Hunter-Randall, David Nathan and Graham Langley. Then, as the train pulled into Rochford, my mobile rang and it was George.

'I wanted to say,' he said, 'that I had no idea that when I came to the Bull's Head last time Dan had the cost of my eight guests deducted from the band's fees. I've told Candy and her guests that they must pay – so you'll be paid.' I was touched by his recollection of such a tiny point and determination to deal with it.

After the train had drawn into Southend Victoria I stood in the rain for a long time talking to my friend. He sounded youthful and completely untouched by the kind of dementia with which he was now being officially – and regularly – credited.

'John Chilton was there at the do,' I said. 'He sent his love.'

'John's a wonderful player,' said George, 'even though he's abandoned his style of suits and looks paler than before. I'd go and sing with him and Wally Fawkes at the White Hart, Drury Lane – they're there every Tuesday night – but Wally doesn't like singers. And John gets a bit annoyed when Wally says, "That was wrong"!'

We talked of other things too. A prized picture donated to Liverpool Institute by my friend had not been 'officially' accepted yet. 'Fuck 'em!' he said (a favourite phrase). 'I'll take it back and give it to the artist's estate. That's all.'

I mentioned how much I'd loved his obituary for Mick Mulligan in the *Daily Telegraph* and the spectacular portrait of the two of them in action that accompanied it. 'Very moving, old friend,' I said. 'And a real rock'n'roll picture! How are you now?'

'Thank you,' said George, 'I'm better generally. And yes, it was a good picture. Though originally they were going to use one of me and Mick sitting with Jimmy Rushing and his two girlfriends.'

I said, 'I can't wait to see you again.'

'Being on-stage . . .' said George, 'and singing the blues is what keeps me alive. I can't wait! We shall embrace.'

Mildly drunk as I was on that early rainy evening it seemed as if the grand old days were back if only for a brief season. 'Bye, bye, darling,' I said.

George's datesheets (faxed through to me by his faithful secretary Shirley) now had as much to do with medical overview as musical or social engagements. Visits on a more or less weekly basis took him to St Mary's Hospital in Praed Street or St Charles in Exmoor Street to monitor his condition with blood and other tests. Checks at colorectoral clinics, at the diabetic endocrinic and ENT centres – all these steered our superstar along the hazardous road designed to lead to continuing health. In between these trips – as well as gigs – came a busy round of social functions and visits, among others, to old friend Andy Garnett in Somerset. Then there were parties and visits to art exhibitions for business and pleasure and to lectures. All these continued to keep George Melly almost as busy as ever.

Soon after, though, came a bad night. On 25 January we had driven down to Hove for a concert at the Old Market Place Theatre, a regular jazz venue which had previously promoted concerts by Humphrey Lyttelton, Stacey Kent and others. Soon after George's arrival, with bookstall and CDs in place in the foyer, I was summoned to his dressing room.

'Here,' said George, 'is a book. You know you need it because your memory is as bad as mine. So every time Diana tells you something you are to write it down – and then you won't forget. See? I've put a little dedication.'

'To be on your person at *all* times' it read and below:

This little book is a useful and acceptable gift from Digby's chum George (Sir George!) to write down what he is told during the day when his mind makes a grasshopper as retentive of information as that creature! Most of what he forgets comes from Diana, whom I will ask to check and read aloud what you or she have written down. Much love – Sir George.'

I wasn't aware of any forgotten instructions from Diana but had to admit that at the end of the evening, when bandleader and star were both tipsy, there were precedents for the situation. 'So thank you,' I said. 'And how are you?'

'Well, the dementia is accelerating – and I'm full of cancer,' George confessed. 'The doctor's given me until the end of July. But I shall go on singing until I can't do so any more.'

The first half of the concert was superb: a planned interview for George with trombonist-broadcaster Campbell Burnap, my old friend, who had made his second name as one of the music's most knowledgeable, approachable and radio-friendly commentators on a seventeen-year show for Jazz FM as well as for the BBC. Campbell had done his homework superbly and the interview would have graced national television. It was full of intimate references, finely researched points and the kind of sympathy for his subject that had made Campbell a highly rated national spokesman for classic jazz.

But when the second half arrived and George made his unsteady way to his chair it was clear that something was wrong. His opening 'Old Rockin' Chair' wandered hopelessly from both lyric and accompaniment and the rambling disconnected announcement that followed bore little relation to our show. The follow-up – a normally spirited version of 'Cakewalkin' Babies from Home' – left the tracks in similar fashion before limping to a conclusion.

George sat there in silence, then began the announcement he had made before. It tailed off to silence and, to my horror, our star began to topple sideways off his chair.

'He's had enough, Dig,' warned Nick Millward from behind his drums. 'Get him off.'

Members of the audience and staff rushed to the stage and George was carried away. What to do? Close the show?

'Ladies and gentlemen,' I said. 'In our first half you heard Campbell Burnap reminding George of a famous evening at Ronnie Scott's when, after considerable celebration, he was unable to continue and John [Chilton] made the famous announcement that "the captain is no longer in charge of his ship". Well,' I continued, 'it seems that we've encountered a similar nautical problem. But with your approval we'll try and keep you happy until our captain is able to return.'

But of course he couldn't and the Half-Dozen valiantly finished the show to an ovation. It was an uncomfortable fifty minutes, however. Had George had a stroke? Or perhaps worse still had he left the building completely?

Once off-stage, I ran to the phone and dialled the West Sussex Hospital in Brighton. Yes, Mr Melly had been brought in. Yes, he was conscious. And now he was down in the Medical Assessment Unit. There was very little doubt that he would be there for the night.

I rang Diana. 'You must get home,' she said. 'We'll take care of the problems tomorrow.'

'I'm staying down here tonight, Dig,' said kindly Campbell, 'with my wife Jenny and some old friends. If he's better tomorrow I'll be glad to take him home.' Which he did. By the following morning, George – who had been badly dehydrated and was consequently placed on a drip – was joking with the star-struck staff and gently enquiring if there were somewhere on the ward he might smoke. Back to mobility he met Campbell and entertained his drivers with stories – and a stop at a handy pub – before being met at the door by Diana, who summarily ushered her vagrant charge back into his domicile with a thank-you nod to his kindly drivers.

It was obvious, however, that George couldn't work the

following night and at six hours' notice beautiful Jacqui Dankworth stepped in for our concert at Holt, Norwich, and stole the show.

'All this is going to make the national press,' predicted Jack Higgins and, as usual, he was right. George's collapse hadn't only made local and national television news (including an interview with Kezzie, his granddaughter) but also appeared widely in both tabloids and serious newspapers. Diana Melly, soon to become the spokesman-commentator for George's medical problems, went on *News at Six* but was happy to report that five minutes after his collapse he was requesting a return to the stage to finish the show.

'We're not doing ourselves any good,' warned Jack. 'People will stop booking George if they think he's dying. From now on keep an eye on him. Make sure he eats before the show – and drinks plenty of water. Otherwise people are simply going to cancel.' And sure enough a day or two later came a worried call from Cole Mathieson, who had welcomed George for decades and was due to host his return to the Concorde, Eastleigh less than two weeks later.

'Will he be all right?' asked Cole.

'Don't worry,' I said. 'I'm sure he will be!'

Which he was. Fortified by friends who bought him food at the club, and Nick Millward, who relentlessly pressed pint-glasses of water into his hand, our star was unfaultable. Before the show I went to see him in the dining-room.

'I know you're fine,' I said, 'and looking after yourself. But have you got everything you need?'

Sitting with his friends, George returned a sweet smile. 'I'm fine,' he said. 'And I find I rather like being looked after.'

Whatever TLC had been administered to our star, it had certainly worked. At the Concorde his voice sounded stronger than ever, as if somehow he might be shouting defiantly at the spectre of mortality. No lines were fluffed, jokes were focused and word perfect and the Half-Dozen and I were astounded.

Just over a week later, on 16 February, much the same wondrous thing occurred, this time at our regular haunt, the Marlowe Theatre, Canterbury, where, with Jacqui, we were due to play *The Sounds of Jazz* show. Beforehand I had received my usual summons to the master's dressing room.

'Have you got your notebook?' he asked. Luckily I had.

'I've got mine too,' said George affectionately. 'See? Here it is. And you see I've arranged it alphabetically.' Sure enough, as the pages turned they were marked 'A' to 'Z' in his favoured black Papermate felt-tip pen.

'But I have something else I want to to do,' he said. 'Another album.'

'Really?' I said.

'Yes,' he replied. 'I want it to be me with guest star Jacqui and on the next page the "award-winning Half-Dozen". And I have an excellent idea for the cover. It might be seven turkeys looking at a coffin [this was the time of the Bernard Matthews bird-flu scandal] and they're saying "'e looks bootiful!"'

I roared with laughter.

'Or indeed,' he continued, 'we could, I daresay, have seven of your players around a gravestone . . .'

'Oh come on!' I said, nonplussed by the courage of my friend.

'Face it, dear chap,' he said, 'I'm dying. But not just yet. First the album.'

'I'll see to it,' I said, though I wasn't sure how.

Once again it was a good concert (George had eaten well and drunk plenty of water) but later the bite of Jameson's whiskey affected our progress a little and loving reminiscences on Bessie Smith stretched one of George's announcements to around fifteen minutes amid audible audience titters. I finished the show with a handy cover-up. 'Well, ladies and gentlemen,' I said, while Jacqui waited patiently in the wings, 'tonight we've been happy to bring you not just a concert but an audience with George Melly.' There was applause. 'Perhaps,' I said to him later, 'we might shorten the announcements a bit. Even though it's so good to hear you talk so passionately about someone you've loved all your life.' George – ever the band singer – nodded compliantly.

Two days later, I had been staying at friend Daphne Shoolman's flat in Hampstead and picked up my mobile in time for a 'Saturday chat' with Jack Higgins. As time had passed Jack and I had become closer. The business in which he had been a dominant figure for almost sixty years occupied him all week and conversations would be brief and devoid of smalltalk, but on Saturday morning he would sometimes pick up the phone for a friendly catch-up conversation.

'Hello, my friend! How are you?'

'Fine, Jack,' I said. 'How good to hear you, lord and master! And how's the weather in Bradwell?'

'Lovely!' he said, 'Crocuses blooming in the garden already. And daffodils too.'

'Spring's on the way, it seems,' I said.

'Global warming probably,' said Jack, ever the realist. 'But I don't need to worry about that.'

'Well, neither will I,' I said. 'But please don't stop yet. Because if you do my career as a park-keeper begins.'

Jack laughed. 'I won't be around for ever. But by the time I've stopped I hope you'll be established in your own right.' The remark bore a hint of tenderness that I found very moving. My friend Jack Higgins was showing – as he sometimes did – his soft side. But whether he could realise his hope was another matter.

'My life is serving my people,' he said. 'And, you know, *The*

Sounds of Jazz show with you, Jacqui and George is about the only thing that's doing anything right now.'

The remark had me thinking. Because for the first time my datesheet was beginning to show alarming gaps. The sad demise of Don Lusher had brought to an end the busy activities of the Best of British Jazz. And, with Don's death, Jack had decided that the Great British Jazz Band had taken one too many body blows too. Neither unit was working any more. And George, like it or not, was slowing down too. One day soon there would have to be some changes made.

But meantime to my astonished delight, an opening had appeared for the last album that George wanted so badly. Paul Adams – of the well-regarded Lake label, up in Cumbria – had begun a programme of new issues in addition to his dedicated reissue of old (and sometimes badly neglected) albums by prominent British bands. Might he, I asked, consider a new Melly album? And Paul, to my delight, had said yes!

George was very happy and within a day had faxed across a list of his choices. After the experiments of the last album, his selections dug back deeply to his musical roots with Mick Mulligan, many of Bessie Smith's most notable standards, traditional favourites like 'Salty Dog' and 'Down In The Dumps', plus fine selections from the Fats Waller cadre. In addition he would read selected extracts from his books and, yes, a brief blues for Mick Mulligan was a good idea too.

On Sunday, 25 February Dominic and I drove to Shepherd's Bush to check keys with George. In the hall, stepdaughter Candy met us. 'Hello,' she said. 'Diana's away at a literary festival so I'm sitting in. He's upstairs and well. But it was a hard day yesterday.'

'Was he ill?' I asked, alarmed.

'No,' said Candy. 'On the contrary. We had to go to an orthodox Catholic memorial service and it was all in Latin. And he kept writing notes to me saying, "Shall I stand up and shout 'It's all bollocks'?'"

Plainly our host had lost none of his rebellious instincts. Seated in the armchair he looked comfortable and was as welcoming as ever. 'I've just heard the most amazing thing on television,' he said. 'Apparently Toulouse-Lautrec had a lover who was on the musical stage. And she used to sing the song that daddies still sing to their children: "Daddy Wouldn't Buy Me a Bow-wow". But APPARENTLY when she sang it on-stage and got to the part about "I've got a little cat and I'm very fond of that!", she lifted her skirt up to her waist. And then when she got to the punchline about "I'd rather have a big bow wow!" she lifted her fist up from the elbow. Isn't that marvellous? Well, shall we check keys?'

The power still in his voice was amazing as we ran through the old blues and vaudeville songs he adored. For one – 'Down in the Dumps' – he reached the line 'Mr Landlord' and remembered how Mick Mulligan had interjected 'Mr Meadmore', George's long-suffering landlord from the beloved old days at Margaretta Terrace where he had been a lodger with Mick Mulligan back at the start of his career. When not establishing comfortable keys for his songs, he ran, as blithely hilarious as ever, through old music-hall routines and gags, including one antiquity from the days of Nestlé's tinned goat's milk: 'The trouble Mr Nestlé and I have/Is getting those goats to sit on them cans!'

Two days later, Diana Melly went on television's *News at Six* again to announce that George Melly was now officially suffering from dementia. Naturally the piece was seen by most of Britain's population, and Jack Higgins's fury mounted. 'Do you want *all* his work cancelled?' he demanded.

On the phone to me Diana was unrepentant and determined. 'I've told Jack,' she said, 'that George has only got months to live anyhow. And in every interview I've said that he can remember words and still sing – even though he doesn't know what day it is. I'm not taking any more shit from Jack. And I've had a letter from the "for dementia" charity thanking me for upping the profile of their campaign.'

Now, it seemed the heat was really on. I wrote twenty basic arrangements for our new album in two days and on 5 March my heroic rhythm section – Craig Milverton, Dominic Ashworth, Len Skeat and Nick Millward – recorded them all in one day. On the way home, an old friend, David Thomas, rang me. 'Dig,' he said, 'I thought you should see something.' He named a prominent national newspaper. 'There's a big article in there about George.'

And a big one it was. Headed 'George got nasty – it wasn't like him', a full-page article dug deep into George's developing condition. In an interview with Diana, some unexpected grievances appeared to rise to the surface. She was reported to have said that 'her grieving had happened when George was diagnosed with cancer' and that 'she was pleased by the dementia diagnosis because she had begun imagining things; is it me?' The article went on to say that she enjoyed being in control for a change and that she could now 'boss him around properly' and that, understandably perhaps, she would omit dates with at least one of his girlfriends, while copying George's diary.

George was reported to say that he was now only happy in his bedroom at home. A pen portrait of George depicted him as bedridden listening unceasingly to Bessie Smith records that he loved. A question about the experience of dementia produced the response that, for George, it was a bore and a nuisance. His only comfort was wife Diana who helped him through the thought-fixations of the night and the imagined fantasies of the day. It was reported that, towards the end of the interview, George had relapsed into mental absenteeism.

This article briefly aroused my anger. But I knew full well that reporters can have a field day with a situation and that articles could steer off course. But the sad quotation that George was 'only happy' in his bedroom stayed in my head. And, sure enough, Diana was on the phone soon after. 'I didn't like that article,' she affirmed, 'there have been more sympathetic ones which you should read. They're on the Internet. Anyhow how shall we get George to the studio tomorrow for the recording session? Shall I put him in a cab?'

Which she did and promptly at 10 a.m. George Melly emerged from his taxi fit and ready to record, once again in Julian's marvellous studio. Amid merciless ribbing – 'where's your book then? Forgotten it! I thought so' – he careered through fourteen titles, shouting the blues like a tiger and joyously careering through a one-take 'Salty Dog' with all the carefree panache of a Bessie Smith and with only brief breaks for cigarettes in the garden and two minute sips of whiskey. At the very end, I suggested my 'Blues for Mick Mulligan' and seated in his chair in the vocal booth George sang:

I went down South – but old Mick Mulligan had gone
It's just a short time – but it feels like oh so long.

As he sang the first line he sobbed and my own eyes momentarily filled with tears too.

'I wonder,' he said ruminatively after the take, 'if I should sing "But it seems so *fucking* long"?'

'I'm not sure,' I said. 'Why don't we try it and see?'

The new performance was more powerful still. 'Which do you like best?' asked my band singer.

'I'm not sure. I think the idea is very moving anyhow. But perhaps the "fucking" gives it an extra emphasis. After all it's nothing new – Kenneth Tynan used it on TV forty years ago now. And of course it's very "you". Why don't we let the producer decide?'

So we left it at that and for an hour sat in the garden, in the gathering dusk, laughing, joking and talking of old and new times until at last the taxi arrived and our visitor made his dignified exit.

The next day Diana rang again. She said that George had been George absolutely mad when he got home, making no sense at all and rude to everybody. In the next ten minutes she opened her heart to me a little and I sympathised with her plight. It seemed as if their mutual roads of excess had not this time – according to the rule of Omar Khayyám – led to their palace of wisdom. And, a day or two later, I witnessed the changes of mood that alter the demeanour of a human being cursed with dementia from day to day. At 8.10 a.m. – very early on the morning of 8 March – George was on the phone to me.

'This is DEFINITELY my last album,' he affirmed. 'So keep the arrangements simple. No "progression" now! Remember what Jelly said – "sweet, soft, plenty rhythm".' The old familiar formula of Jelly Roll Morton still sang through George Melly's stout heart.

CHAPTER THIRTEEN

Sadness in Great Ones

The next day, while Julian and I were mixing George's vocals at the studio, a new voice arrived on the telephone. This was Michael Woods, an old friend of George who had collaborated with him on a book *Paris and the Surrealists*.

'I found George sitting outside his house at 10 a.m. this morning,' he said, 'waiting to go to Southport.'

'Oh dear,' I said. 'That's not until tomorrow. Everyone knew.'

'But that's the problem,' said Michael. 'There's nobody there. Diana's away in Bagnor. The people living with him – Chris and Tina – are occupational therapists and are out at work all day – and often they're out at night too. So there's no one there to see he gets his medication at the proper times; often he takes everything at one go last thing at night, if he remembers at all. And of course he's not eating properly. So I've been going in – and apparently he's been hallucinating again. On Monday Diana and I are going to meet to discuss the matter of qualified carers going into the house at regular intervals.'

The following day we played Southport at the Talbot Hotel and George looked well enough. 'Hello, Grasshopper,' he said. 'Forgotten your book again?'

'Sorry!' I said, not knowing quite what for, and went to finish our sound check. Later I was called up to the Master's bedroom and found him snuggled up in bed.

'Hello,' I said. 'I've been worried about you!'

'Why?'

'I'm afraid that you need more help.'

'Bollocks,' said George briefly. 'I've had people coming in from all sides.' And, whether or not that was true, by the following Wednesday arrangements had been made and qualified carers – said Diana's voice, live on Radio 4 on Wednesday, 14 March – were now, sure enough, securely in place at home.

Meantime, the night after Southport, we had played a big benefit which I'd organised for George's former drummer Eddie Taylor at 100 Oxford Street. The Great British Jazz Band, Humphrey Lyttelton with special guest, Scott Hamilton, and Ron Russell's All Stars had all played. And George had sung with a re-formed Feetwarmers band, including John Chilton and Wally Fawkes, along with Nick Dawson, Len Skeat and Allan Ganley. Despite a lengthy dedication to Stan Greig, whose benefit he had decided it might be instead, George nevertheless stopped the show, just as he had done thirty years earlier, as I watched him sing 'Shave 'em Dry'. It was still easy to think that very little had changed.

But after that there was silence for almost a fortnight. Fuelled by the medical news, I began to wonder seriously if we had seen the last of our hero and determined to ring. Apparently he had appeared on television with Diana talking about his condition. But then the phone rang and it was Diana.

'Hello, Digby,' she said. 'I have something I want to discuss with you. A film company, Walkergeorge Films, want to make a documentary about George's life and his current problems. And they want to film you, him and the Half-Dozen at the

Bull's Head in Barnes on Saturday. We think it might be his last performance! So we need to set rates with you and the band.' Fair as always.

My only hope was that the documentary – as an edition of Melvyn Bragg's *South Bank Show* had done a week or so previously for Humphrey Lyttelton – would be a celebration of George's life rather than a documentary about his current malaise. And a few hours later the show's producer assured me that that would indeed be the case. 'Would there be interviews,' I asked 'with his old associates, Wally Fawkes, Humph, John Chilton, perhaps George Webb and others? Old footage? Artists like Maggie Hamblyn who had painted him? Radio and television presenters or other cultural colleagues who had worked with him?' My questions were all answered with assurances; yes, these plans were already made.

Then an hour later, on the phone came George. 'I'll let you talk to him,' said Shirley, his secretary.

'Hello there,' said George, 'I wanted to ask how the new album was going. And to ensure "sweet soft, plenty rhythm", you know.'

'All, old friend,' I said, 'will be exactly as you wish it.'

'I haven't heard it yet of course,' he said.

'I know. We've had a brief hold-up as Julian has had a bout of illness. He's actually had quite a bad few weeks. But it'll be mixed soon and I'll make sure that you get a full copy of the vocal tracks, even if the horns haven't been put on yet.'

'Fine,' said George. 'And, by the way, it occurred to me that, if this album is released after I'm dead, then it very well might sell a lot. Then of course it may not. But I wanted to make certain that the band and its leader make a nice lot of money from the royalties. Everything at this end is taken care of. But it would be nice for the orchestra to do well – and they deserve it.'

'Thank you,' I said, very moved.

We continued talking for a while and then, 'I'll see you Saturday,' said my friend. 'Michael will bring me to the Bull's Head.'

'Might Diana be there?' I asked. 'Or Babs. And how is Babs?'

'She's fine,' said George, 'though I haven't seen her in some time. Craigie, the man she's been looking after, has died now as you may know. But I shall see her when I go and visit Andy Garnett next week.'

'That'll be nice,' I ventured.

'Well, I don't know,' said George, ever cautious of a stock reaction. 'Basically, it's just two old bores waiting for the other one to finish talking so that the other one can have a turn. But it'll be nice to see Babs. Diana is having a tough time with me now.'

'I think Diana has a need to feel needed,' I offered.

'I think so too,' said George. 'By the way, have you read John Chilton's book *Hot Jazz Warm Feet*?'

'It just arrived today, with a new consignment of mine from my publisher Ann Cotterrell at Northway. What did you think?'

'Well,' said George, 'it's OK I think. But he's too nice about everybody. There's no details of the screaming furious face-to-face rows we had. Or of the people in the Feetwarmers that we didn't get on with. None of that. It's all a bit comfortable.' In retrospect I found this to be an ungenerous assessment.

'Not enough "owning up" perhaps?' I suggested.

'Exactly,' George concurred. 'Well, bye, bye, darling. I'll see you tonight.'

'Saturday,' I reminded him.

'Saturday,' he said. 'For sure! Bye, bye, dear. Bye!' The voice, as he rang off, sounded as young, as intimate, as full of spring promises as the burgeoning trees up and down the street where he lived.

Meantime, Mike, George's new minder, had texted me. Should George bring CDs and books to the job? This was something we didn't normally do as sales at the Bull's Head were usually unaccountably poor, but I was glad of the help and all my own stocks had now been returned to the Mellys. 'Lovely,' I texted back. 'But you will need to count what you bring. Make a list. And bring a float of £20 with you for change.'

So Saturday rolled around: Boat Race day 2007. And consequently when I arrived at the Bull's Head, Barnes, with clarinettist Tim Huskisson, the pub – and most of Barnes itself – was packed with celebrants, many of them in the latter stages of alcoholic fulfilment. I wedged my way through the smoky crowds and into the jazz room ('sponsored by Yamaha') to be greeted by the familiar hush that surrounds a TV interview. Diana Melly, dressed to elegant perfection, was at the bar, surrounded by lighting men and cameras, conducting an interview. Anxious not to become a visual disturbance, I hurried to the back of the room and outside to the rear courtyard where I found altoist Peter King and Len Skeat safely out of vision in conversation and joined them until a new figure materialised. This was Mike with a kingly summons. 'When you're clear . . .' he said, 'George would like a word in the bar.'

Through I went to find George, a triumphant scarlet in his kaftan, surrounded by cameras and friends.

'Helloooooooo,' he said genially. 'Come and sit down.'

'How are you?' I asked, as I put my arm around him.

'As well as can be expected,' said George, 'under the circum- stances. Diana is here, so I have to be on my best behaviour. No jokes, no showing off – just singing.'

'That's fine,' I said, 'that's your very strongest point anyhow.'

'And,' said my friend, 'I've only had one whiskey!' He refused another and launched into his familiar, though good-natured, verbal onslaught on one of the performers who occasionally aroused his competitive ire.

'Is this the man I'm thinking it is?' said Mike, looking pained. 'I've heard about this for months!'

'I think so,' I said. But then, aware of a camera-cum-soundman at our shoulder, I steered the conversation to a more positive topic noting a distinct teeter as talk proceeded. Dementia, it seemed, might be taking a more serious hold.

'How was the opening of the Surrealist exhibition?' I asked.

'Good,' said George. 'But I had to tell Alan Yentob off. I said, "You started off by making great programmes. But now if you don't fill in your lottery tickets you must be a great fool. I'm going to call my lawyer and get you around to the office and sue you if you don't."' It seemed that his mind was wandering and we were switching subjects with disturbing speed. Then George took my arm.

'But I have a second thing to say. If this record takes off, as I said – and it may do, it may not – when I'm dead, I want the members of the orchestra and its leader to get a good royalty!'

'That really is very sweet,' I said, omitting the phrase 'under the circumstances' but touched by the fact he was re-enforcing this point, 'thank you.' And I kissed him on the cheek to be greeted by the old flirtatious *moue* that followed any such action. 'Now I must go and get my cornet and warm up.'

Back in the Bull's Head jazz room, the audience was already busily filing in. Nervous and out of practice, I handed out the music to the five remaining musicians who this night were to make up the Half-Dozen – Tim, pianist Nick Dawson, Chris Gower, Len and Nick – and warmed up lip, stomach and mind with a healthy slug of Dr Smirnoff's prescription. Wandering back into the room momentarily, I found Diana Melly, seated dead centre in the front row looking radiant. I used a standard joke.

'Couldn't,' I asked, 'you get somewhere closer?' She smiled, looking happy and relaxed.

'How did the interview go?' I said.

'Fine. They asked me lots of questions. Including, "why don't I go to all of George's gigs?"'

'What did you say?' I asked.

'Because I've got lots of other better things to do.'

'Good answer,' I said.

But then it was time to begin. To the packed room, 'Good evening!' I said. 'Tonight we are here to celebrate a very special event, the filming of part of a George Melly documentary. And we are privileged to be joined by his wife. Please acknowledge the presence of Mrs Diana Melly!' There was applause as she waved. 'And very soon, the reason we are all here – and have been treading the boards for the past five years – Mr George Melly himself!'

The room was packed as the Half-Dozen swung into action and soon George was at the front awaiting his cue. Helped by Mike, he made his stately way to centre stage, pausing regally to shake my hand before he took his seat.

'Old rockin' chair's got me . . .'

The power in his voice was still amazing. Our back-chat patter proceeded smoothly enough and at the end, following a top E flat, Louis Armstrong style from my cornet, the audience rose to its feet. Diana was smiling. And regularly, as the set proceeded, the cameraman skilfully panned between the two of them as well as following the solos of the Half-Dozen. This felt like a good night.

And it was. Shots completed, Diana left at half-time ('Now I can tell dirty jokes,' said George with a wicked gleam) and, although the vocals took their own eccentric course at one or two points, there was a great deal of useable footage at the end and the crew headed by Sally George and Katie Buchanan from Walkergeorge Films were delighted. So was the audience who gave our star a deserved standing ovation as 'Nuts' came to an end.

'It's nice how you all look after him,' said Sally.

I was always disarmed by the compliment, occasionally offered by friendly onlookers. 'It's a pleasure and a privilege,' I said.

The day after was Easter and I took the opportunity to spend a couple of relaxed days with friends. Then on Tuesday, as the Easter weekend turned back to the everyday business of the year, the phone rang and it was Jack Higgins.

'Oh there you are!' he said. 'How was Saturday?'

'Fine,' I said. 'George was on fine form. The crowd was packed. And we had a standing ovation. I've got lots of money for you.'

'Good,' said Jack. 'Send it all off! I'll deduct the VAT and George's fee and send you the rest. The usual one-and-nine.'

'Fine,' I said laughing. 'And how was Easter?'

'Well, quiet,' said Jack. 'But all right!'

'I'll look forward to seeing you. Take good care!'

'Goodbye, my friend,' he said.

But then the phone rang again and it was George. 'I'm very cross with you,' he said in mock ire. 'Did you tell Mike that we shouldn't sell at the end of the gig?'

'No,' I said. 'But I did tell him he might have to help as we were busy with the film company.'

'The film company,' said George, 'is there to film. Your job is to sell. And we might have sold a lot more had you been there.' It was nice to know that I was indispensable on occasion!

'I'm very sorry.'

'I'm glad to hear you say that. And I'll end with a west-country motif. Had you been caught by some country constable – shall we say scrumping apples – you would have been led back to the scene of the crime and given a thick ear.'

I laughed, still amazed at the diversity of his thought processes. 'I'm sorry, as I said. And please give Mike my love.' It seemed likely that we were all coming in for a little bit more of his censure. But quickly I shook off the feelings of regret.

Then Diana Melly was on the phone. 'What are we to do with George on future gigs? Who's going to look after him?'

That day, a new email arrived. Diana wanted to discuss arrangements for getting George to gigs, how George needed help with dressing and that, as he now needed a minder, another room would have to be booked at gigs.

The next morning I rang Diana, full of sympathy at her situation. We spoke at some length about George's plight.

'I only have a few minutes as I have to take George to the hospital. But now we've agreed that George needs a full minder at all times. So I'm arranging two single rooms, and Mike, or Chris who lives with us, will be with him. And I'm very concerned that at no time does he turn into a totem-pole for ridicule.'

'I absolutely agree,' I said. 'And we'll take care of that.'

'He is getting absolutely impossible to live with,' said Diana. 'The other day he started talking to me about Mannie Shinwell – remember him? He was one of the Attlee government. And although he lived to be a hundred he's been dead for twenty years. George started talking about him digging a coalmine in someone's back yard just because they were rich. And he said, "It's last month." I said, "George – I don't think so." And he started to shout at me.'

I remembered the fatigues and frustrations that go with attending invading sickness; I had had them even with my own mother. 'It must be absolute hell,' I said. 'I know a little of how you feel.'

'What is this,' she asked, 'about George getting a lawyer to get Len Skeat to fill in his lottery forms?'

'Oh, that comes from an old argument. Len tends to get under George's skin as he likes to try and top him and George of course is very bright and tends to resent the competition. So months ago he told Len that if he had regular numbers and they came up – and Len hadn't filled his form in, especially as he was once very rich and isn't any more – he would have great cause for regret. And it's turned into a sort of mantra, with a germ of truth in it, to be fair. That sometimes happens when people begin to approach senility.'

'He's not senile,' returned Diana. 'He has vascular dementia. The Society gets very upset if people say "senile". Humphrey Lyttelton could be called senile because he's old. The word just means "old".'

'Well,' I said, 'Humph certainly isn't senile. He's in fine shape and as sharp as a tack. And it's only a word. But I've always understood the word to mean that old people's mental capacity is reducing.'

'Look it up in a dictionary,' she said.

'Certainly,' I said and made for my Collins office volume. 'According to this definition, it is "mentally or physically weak or infirm on account of old age".'

'Well, that's wrong,' said Diana. 'Look it up in some others. I have to take George to the hospital now.'

'OK,' I said. 'Let's not argue about it. Have a good day. Goodbye!'

Two days later a note from Diana arrived, scribbled on the back of a textbook explanation of dementia in which text had been highlighted for my benefit, explaining why the term 'senility' should not be used. She had become a devoted sympathiser to the cause.

Over the next few days it became increasingly clear that

Diana's campaign to publicise George's decline had worked her into the public's consciousness. However, one less-than-sympathetic onlooker had unfairly accused her of 'banging on' about the matter. At numerous venues I was constantly asked not just how George was, but also whether he had ceased working, or had even died. And it occurred to me again that, given my friend's wish to perform until the end, her well-meant campaign might not be encouraging that situation to remain a reality.

Jack Higgins felt so too. Our conversations had become those of old friends.

'I don't know what she's up to,' said Jack. 'But you might be interested in a chat I had with her last Sunday, at 8.30 at night.'

'What was that?' I asked.

'Some time ago George was offered a part in a film; just making an appearance to sing a song. Nothing came of it. But Diana rang and said, "George is convinced that he's making a film and that he's going to play Jesus in it. And consequently he's growing a beard." Can you imagine that? Given George's views on religion, I would have thought that an appearance as the anti-Christ might be more suitable.'

We laughed together. But reports from his west London home were becoming more limited as the days went by. Mike remained a regular visitor and guardian to look after George, along with his in-house guest Chris, who was now to take on some of the driving chores. Then on Wednesday, 18 April, just after I'd come back from an enjoyable but boozy governors' meeting at Southend High School, at 10.30 a.m. the phone rang and it was Diana again. She sounded disturbed and the undertone of hysteria that had occasionally entered her voice of late was present again.

'Digby,' she said. 'I want to talk to you!'

'What can I do?' I said.

'George is completely mad now! You've heard that he's grown a beard? And you know the story?'

'Yes,' I said.

'Well,' she said, 'I think it's impossible for him to go on. Now he thinks he's John the Baptist. He can hardly walk from his bedroom to the bathroom. He's even afraid of the stairs now. So he would need help to get from the wheelchair on to the stage. How's he going to do that? And Chris, and his partner, who are living with him, are occupational therapists and they're convinced that he'll be nothing but a laughing stock on-stage. Look at the Bull's Head last week.' Her voice rose.

'I think everybody knows now that George's performing days are numbered. The publicity that's surrounded that issue means that I'm constantly being asked if he's even able to appear on-stage. I know you have his best interests at heart, Di, but I wonder if his ambition to sing until the end of his days is being threatened by that.'

'But during the last ten days things have got much worse. And I need your support, Digby,' she continued.

'You always have my support, Di. Nobody wants George to appear a fool on-stage. And the moment that happens we have to stop. But meantime your first refuge is Jack – Jack Higgins.'

'I don't want to tell Jack that he can't perform any more.'

'There's nothing to stop you doing that,' I said. 'George has never signed a single contract with Jack. They've worked together on a handshake – always. So Jack hasn't got a leg to stand on in legal terms if he chose to take a stand, which is very unlikely. And I think you have to say when enough is enough.' I was aware that aligning myself wholeheartedly with Diana's view might turn me into a graceless pig-in-the-middle, roasted on the spit between artist, agent and wife.

'But I don't want the venues suing me,' said Diana, 'for breach of contract.'

'They'd never do that. Illness is a sad thing, but unavoidable. But how about his minders – Mike, Chris and his partner?'

'They all think it's time he should stop,' she said. The recurring thought crossed my mind and I entered dangerous territory.

'But how much are they there?' I asked. 'Chris and his partner have a day-time job, don't they? So do they perhaps just see him when he's tired in the evening?'

'Tired?' returned Diana. 'He's not just tired in the evening, Digby. He never gets out of bed. Last evening I went up to see him and he asked me when lunch would be ready.'

'It's a sad thing for him – and for all of us. But in the end the decision belongs with you.'

'But,' she said again, 'I need your support, Digby. You and other friends.' She sounded distressed and I felt sorry for her and the inevitable trauma she was struggling with.

'Well,' I said. 'Why don't I come round tomorrow? To see the man. Remember that I'm still really an outsider. But I can talk to him and see for myself what's happening. Then you and I must have a talk and see where we go from here.'

'OK,' she said reluctantly. 'But ring me before 4.30. I'm going out and George is going to an art exhibition with Mike Pointon.'

'That sounds hopeful,' I offered.

'But he thinks he's opening it,' she responded. 'And that was three weeks ago.'

'Never mind. Let's talk tomorrow. And don't worry too much. Sleep well.'

But deep down I was unhappy. At one side of my stage sat an agent who continued to book an old act – and friend – because he wanted them to do so. At the other stood a distressed woman with her own deep emotions; who clearly loved her husband of almost fifty years, but who was understandably exasperated by him and who seemed (quite admirably) to want to see his career come to a halt before invidious insanity took hold in the public view.

The only answer seemed to be to go back to west London.

CHAPTER FOURTEEN

Farewell Old King

Thursday, 19 April 2007 dawned bright and sunny, a full-blooming spring morning. It would be a good day in the main; I was due to record my second show for the new radio station theJazz before my trip to see George. But, despite the optimism of the promises of spring and a visit to the newly flourishing radio station which played jazz music to the nation 24 hours a day, I was still beset with doubts and concern: for George's future, my own and my beloved band. This could mark the end of our career and what was left of my income. Not for the first time I began to cross my fingers for a Premium Bond win. And strangely, there was one on the mat – for £100! I accepted this small gesture from a kindly deity with gratitude, but was still far from sure about what to do.

Perhaps a second opinion might be a good idea? I rang my constant support Dominic Ashworth whose creative playing and fine judgement had turned him into a close friend in the Half-Dozen. His wife Catherine, wide awake at 7.40 a.m., was a welcoming voice.

'No problem,' she said. 'He's not up yet. But I think he's free, though he has a job tonight. And I could pick up the girls from school.' So Dominic agreed that we would meet that evening to – in Fagin's latter-day words – 'review the situation'.

But meantime I decided to call Diana Melly. 'Hi, Di,' I said.

'Hello, Digby. I think it's a very good idea that you come around and see George. But you know – what you said last night about his being tired in the evening – that's simply not true. You don't live here with him.'

'No, of course I don't,' I said.

'And,' said Diana, 'I've had Jack on the phone this morning. He suggested that he should speak to George's doctor and I said "No, Jack! Of course he won't talk to you!"' Jack had then, apparently, gone on to suggest that George should be in a home, outraging Diana, though it was probably not a serious suggestion as Jack both wanted to help and had a natural agent's reluctance to retire his acts.

Promptly at 7.30 a.m. Dominic and I arrived at George's house to be greeted by a chorus of canine welcome from the yap-yaps and Tina, who introduced herself as one of George's in-house carers, and welcomed us up to the sitting-room where we sat together to talk about things.

'He is getting very frail,' she said, 'and I think there's been a quite serious decline over the last ten days or so. He only seems secure in his room and even has a big job with the stairs.'

'There are special nurses who look after people with dementia and such,' said Dominic. 'Do they come in?'

'They do,' said Chris. 'But generally Diana sees them – and they also help with her own problems. Myself and my partner help people with physical and mental health problems. We've been here since last September and seen cases like this before. We take him his food and a cup of tea and keep an eye on him. But nowadays he's reluctant even to take his medication.'

'Should we pay a call?' I said.

Chris led us up the stairs and tapped on the door.

'George,' he said. 'Are you awake? Digby and Dominic are here.'

'Send them up,' came the regal command and Dominic and I tiptoed in. George was curled up in bed, a dramatically shrunken figure with a growth of white beard, wrapped in a shroud of sheets. The light was low and there was a drab feeling of mortality surrounding the antique bed, dusty furniture and old, once-challenging artefacts that stood in the room. Among them, on the floor, lay a pile of books, the unwanted remnants left by a book dealer who had called that day to assess valuable volumes and take them away for sale.

'Now,' he said, 'I have several things to say to you!' And proceeded with a focused monologue covering many now-familiar areas: my non-appearance at the Bull's Head sales ten days before (finger wagging); the need for our band to play far more with 'sweet soft, plenty rhythm'; Len Skeat's non-compliance to fill in his lottery forms despite financial penury; his determination that – should his final album take off – our band should receive at least a generous portion of the royalties. 'You're a witness!' he confirmed, pointing to Dominic.

When he came to a halt I leaned forward. 'But how are you?' I asked.

'Well, you can see!' returned George spiritedly. 'I'm filled with cancer – from here to here. Vile fluids are leaving my body by day and night. And I'm dying. That's pretty obvious, isn't it?'

Then Dominic – compassionate and ever-ready to listen – leaned forward. 'But, George,' he said. 'Do you want to carry on? Singing? And playing with the band?'

The response was immediate. 'Of course I do! It's the only thing I live for!'

Downstairs again, we talked to Chris and Tina. The worries over out-of-town appearances were reiterated; the concept of a 'farewell concert' briefly discussed, though it seemed to me we had more urgent matters to think of now.

On the way home I read two letters which had been handed to me by Chris on arrival at George's house: cautionary warnings over the risks of the future from Michael Woods, his minder most days and, more unusually, a statement typed up by Diana, dated and signed – intriguingly – as 'George Melly or George Melly'. In Mick Mulligan's words, 'there was still a lot going on in that ageing nut.'

But on the way back Dominic was his usual sensible self. 'What we have to deal with, Dig,' he said, 'is an old man who's dying but simply wants to perform. There mustn't be contention; it's gone beyond who's done what or said what. We simply have to do the best for George. If I were Diana, I know what I'd do. But we have to consider a couple of important issues. One: should we simply suggest that he just sings on open invitation around London with us, so that the mountains must come to Mahomet rather than George feeling obliged to make those long trips? And if he does carry on with those, are we in legal trouble if George dies in one of our cars?' This was indeed a thought to reckon with.

The next morning I rang Michael urgently. For some months he had been visiting George: washing his hair, listening to the frequently rambling conversations or just sitting to hold his hand. Sometimes the pressures had been considerable.

'George said, "I've lost something under the bed. Can you look for it?" So I said, "What is it?" and George said, "I won't know until I see it!" So there am I under the bed pulling out everything that was there and every time he says, "That's not it." So finally I'm sweating and breathless and I said, "George, I can't do this any more. I'm exhausted." And George said, "Well, I'll just have to find something else to clean my CDs with." And it was on his bedside table.'

Michael knew his stuff and was currently co-writing a book on neurosurgery. He explained to me the risks that George was now facing: lack of blood flow to central brain cells; the pressures on his heart because of his physical decline; the impending threats of a heart attack, a stroke or even death in a car or on-stage.

'So,' I asked, 'would you be prepared to travel with George to the out-of-town engagements he still has in his book?'

'No,' said Mike, 'I've had them in the book, I know. But now I wouldn't be prepared.'

The next morning – full of worries – I faxed this letter to our agent.

My dear Jack,

We've agreed that we should stay in close touch over the matter of George and following two telephone conversations from Diana on Wednesday and Thursday I visited [George] yesterday (with Dominic Ashworth my friend and guitarist in the Half-Dozen whose opinion I value) to talk to his in-house minders Chris and Tina and to George. On arrival I was handed the two letters which accompany this fax, and which I thought you should see.

There is no doubt that our dear friend is very ill now. To call him 'frail' would be putting it kindly (his body is wilfully shrunken by the cancer) and his conversation repetitive and eccentric – although to be fair the matter of the film and his potential role as Jesus wasn't mentioned! I asked him how he was and received the direct answer 'Look at me – I'm riddled with cancer from top to bottom!' which sadly I am sure he is. We talked for fifteen minutes or so before Dominic asked the direct question: 'Do you want to keep working – and singing with the band?' to which George replied an emphatic 'Yes – it's the only thing that keeps me going.'

I'm sure it is too. But Chris and Tina – who are qualified occupational therapists – are very concerned about his out-of-town work, as of course is Diana. Apparently he regularly declines to take his prescribed medication (the side effects are hard for him to cope with) and has a job even leaving his room. I had a long and serious conversation about the future and what could – or should – be done.

Our conclusion after the talk was that there is a problem to deal with. It was suggested that George should only undertake London work from now on. And although I pointed out that this presents huge implications in professional/contractual terms I must say that I can see their reasons. I am also sure that a full-time minder would now be necessary for any such extended trips, should they occur.

One conclusion was that George's GP – or in my view his specialists – should be consulted over the situation and professional medical advice taken over whether travelling is still practical. But we also agreed that George's declared wishes to perform for as long as possible should be fully respected until his time has come. Plainly his second home is the stage.

I do think we need to talk, old friend. I know that a knee-jerk reaction would be to say 'Right! We'll cancel all his work from now on. That's it.' But to do so would be to confine him to his tiny bedroom (and probably the hospital) until the Reaper arrives, which is a dismal fate for a performer who still wishes to sing and has declared that 'that's what keeps him going!' I feel sure that neither Diana, Chris, Tina nor any other of his current close associates would wish that situation on him either.

Another point to be raised is that – as you will note from the last line of Diana's dated document signed by George – our position, amid this situation, is a potentially questionable one. For you George – as well as a friend and colleague of decades – is also a professional client. For me – as well as a hero, musical kindred and friend – he is still an occasional source of work! As such we are open to the possible accusation of flogging an old horse who – though not yet demised – is certainly very far from well now. Of course this is not the case, but I think we need to consider any such potential viewpoint with understanding rather than an unnecessarily defensive attitude and deal with it with love for an old and sick friend, compassion and as much constructive help as possible. George is now a very ill old trouper; those around him are under tremendous stress and the situation is a complicated one.

We must talk of course. And I have at the moment no immediate conclusions to offer – beyond the suggestion that we seek definitive medical judgment on George's ability to travel and then, dependent on that, take the necessary steps to make sure that he is taken proper care of, should the answer be 'yes'. (I should add one important point; that Mike – his principal minder – is not prepared to risk the problems inherent in long journeys if this should be the case). If 'no' then we must look at the situation again.

I'm copying this letter to Diana, Chris and Tina.

As ever, your junior client,

Digby

It wasn't long before Jack was on the phone. 'I need something,' he said, 'from a doctor! I've explained to Diana that I have no wish to put George in a bad situation. But as co-director of Man Woman and Bulldog, I have both legal and contractual obligations.'

I understood perfectly. So next, I wrote to Diana.

Dear Di,

Following my visit to [George] last night and a useful talk with Tina, Chris and the Master I thought you would wish to see this letter faxed to Jack this a.m. I have also passed to him the signed document from yourself and the letter from Michael.

Jack has been on the phone very quickly to say that initially he will need signed documentation from George's GP if – after due consultation – George is pronounced 'unfit for travel'. In short a 'sick note'. He needs to know about this as soon as possible and I would suggest you talk to him when you can, as I gather you may have already made contacts and enquiries in this direction.

I've also had a long talk with Michael who has advised me that he would not be prepared to travel with George to out-of-town engagements because of health risks of which he seems to be well informed and fully aware. An initial thought – which we should discuss I think – is that my band may therefore no longer be able to transport George in his enhanced condition for both practical and (possibly) legal reasons. However if qualified medical care could be found – even at some expense – I feel that George's joy in performing should be gratified as long as he is able to do so competently and with dignity and that transport should be considered accordingly.

Hope to talk soon,
Digby

But we weren't to talk soon; I heard nothing from Diana for the remainder of the day but meantime contacted Paul Jones and Georgie Fame to see how they might feel about stepping in for George.

Paul – ever the courteous gentleman – was quick to reply. Within a couple of hours he was on the phone. 'I'm sorry to hear the news, Digby,' he said. 'We'll talk later. Just now I'm on my way to Newark.' And next morning we did indeed talk. Paul was sympathetic and declared himself happy to fulfil a few dates even though he was busy with his Blues Band, the Manfreds and other commitments.

Later, however, I was worried about George and decided to give a quick ring. Diana picked up the phone.

'Di,' I said. 'It's Dig! I just rang up to see how he is.'

'Much the same as ever,' said Di. Her voice sounded cool. 'But I must say, Digby, that I was disappointed with your reaction to our conversation of ten days ago. Do you remember that?'

'Yes, of course I do,' I said.

She went on to say she felt I had only responded because two men, Chris and Mike, had stepped in and that this was a somewhat chauvanist response.

'That's it!' I thought – she obviously had the same idea and the phones went down together.

I was shaking with anger and took ten minutes off for deep breaths. Then with hands still unsteady, I wrote this.

Dear Diana,

Having had a cup of tea – and cooled off! – I would wish to apologise for my part in our somewhat heated exchange. I have no wish to quarrel and have indeed been very grateful for your help in band matters in the past. With George as ill as he is there is plainly no reason to consider anything other than his welfare.

However, I would (gently) make the following points. One, my visit to George this week was prompted solely by your conversation of Tuesday evening and my concern for him; not by the intervention of either Mike Woods or Chris – both of whose role in George's recent decline I have been only vaguely aware. To accuse me of the – somewhat tired – cliché of chauvinism is both inaccurate and invidious. I have regarded you as my principal contact at all times – whether in or away from the house – and my occasional silences have been prompted principally by the fact that, reasonably often, I can't get hold of you.

I also feel it necessary to assure you that my sole concern – as you might (I presume) have gathered from my letter to Jack Higgins yesterday – is purely for George's best interests. He has been a considerable personal inspiration to me for decades and working with him has been, in general, a complete joy. However, as you would have heard – had you been present on Wednesday – neither I, nor my band, have the slightest wish to work for or with him for one moment longer than George wishes to do so, though Chris, Tina, Dominic and I have all agreed that his continued wish to perform for as long as possible should be respected wherever this may be practical.

I am perfectly happy to discuss all or other of the above matters with you at any time and hope that we may now resume friendly and rational relations.

Later, an email arrived from Diana, explaining that doctors' letters were being made available and that all away jobs should be cancelled and promoters told that letters would be coming. She went on to say that George would be driven to local jobs in future, with Michael in attendance, and that she couldn't speak to Jack after his outburst, but that I could, if I wanted to, tell him to cancel jobs on Monday. It was signed with love.

It had been a bad and upsetting exchange all round and I went out and got very drunk. Very drunk indeed. Next morning, wandering dimly round the house I found pictures on the floor and my grandfather clock halfway across the floor. Luckily I'd been sick outside.

So I was glad of Jack's bellowed pep-talk on the phone. 'First of all I can't get you! And two, stop being so fucking emotional. This is business. We don't get Paul Jones yet. We need the facts! Facts first! This is business! Business – remember! I can't do anything without that medical evidence. And once I've got that we move on to stage two – if and when it's necessary. So keep your eye on things. I've got contracts to meet – and obligations. So stop going on an emotional trip – it's not necessary.' The barked instructions were like a breath of much needed fresh air. But it was impossible to shake the feeling of depression that grew as the weekend progressed. Clearly the situation had been getting on top of me and I began to understand how Diana must feel. Listening dully to my new show through Sky television on theJazz for the first time, the screen proclaimed: 'Digby Fairweather! – Further scheduled information unknown.' All too true, I thought.

As my 61st birthday approached, another article appeared in the *Daily Mail*: quotations from George about his terminal illness: 'I don't fear death,' he said, 'I'm a fatalist. Although I would rather death came as a shock to me. I've always said I wanted to die coming off-stage with the applause in my ears or of a terminal stroke on a river bank with two trout by my side.'

Soon after Diana called. Happily our spat seemed to be forgotten. It had been decided that George would sing at his next two jobs – at Worcester, then Newark. Mike and Chris would accompany him and mini-cabs would transport him. And a benefit was to be arranged for the 'for dementia' charity quite soon, for which George would sing. Then Mike was on the phone. 'I'll help with George and travel with him when I can,' he said, 'although he may need a lung drained over the next week or so.'

But gradually the dark clouds seemed to be clearing. First of all, Thursday, the day after my birthday, 25 April, Jack Higgins began talking to Diana again. He told me that he had called her, saying 'Don't get emotional on me!' I have to get things straight in our business dealings. And Digby and Jacqui Dankworth are involved too and we have to think of them.' The two of them agreed that, unavoidably, George's days were rapidly coming to an end. 'We have to talk to the venues,' Jack emphasised to me later. 'One at least will take the show without George. And give me Paul Jones's number. I'll talk to him.' My fax machine whirred into action.

Then, early next morning, came another call from Diana. She was at full speed. 'I'll be driving to Worcester,' she said, 'along with George, Mike, Chris and Tina. The five of us will book into a separate hotel. And the benefit looks like being 10 June. George will sing and hopefully George Webb will play – and maybe Kenny Ball will help out too.' She was full of optimism. 'The film company have had their offer taken up by the BBC,' she continued, 'so all the musicians will get their proper fee. And we intend to help George to sing for as long as possible – even though he sometimes seems to think I'm trying to stop him. But realistically, Digby, he won't be able to do anything after July. I'm sure of that.'

Then on the following Thursday the telephone rang and it was George Webb.

George Webb! At approaching ninety, the founder of

Britain's jazz revival and leader of Britain's first authentic New Orleans band was already a legend. As agile as a diminutive bantamweight boxer, sharp as a box of tacks, and still leading his band with the same irresistible vigour that he did in 1944, he was the most vivid testimony to everlasting youth that I knew of. Only a month or so previously his Band of Brothers had packed the 100 Club with over three hundred disciples.

'Hello, Dig,' he said. 'Yesterday I popped over to Shepherd's Bush to see George and Diana. I nearly came away in tears. Poor old George! When you've been mates for decades, shared jokes and laughter – and music of course! And now he's rambling; talking about his dreams . . . and of course the cancer is all the way through him now. It's so sad.'

'But,' continued this marvellously youthful leader, 'we have to get this benefit going! Kenny's going to play. And so will my Band of Brothers. And yours? And we have to get advertising the gig fast – it's very soon. So you get in touch with Diana and we'll get the deadlines for the publicity for *The Jazz Guide*, Mary Greig's *Jazz in London* and of course my pals at *Just Jazz* [Britain's shiniest monthly devoted to classic jazz] will help too.'

We set to work and George was on the phone daily to get things rolling.

Then Diana called. 'The Society,' she said, 'will be co-ordinating the publicity if that's all right! I've been in touch with Sir Paul McCartney and Van Morrison's people and if things are right they may well drop in. And, yes, we should ask Paul Jones too . . .' This really began to sound like an event but just for now George and I watched in wonder as – over the next month – every seat was sold.

Our next date in early May was to be next door to the home of Sir Edward Elgar; the beautiful Huntingdon Hall in Worcester – an antique place of worship converted to a concert hall, for which the audience sat in pews (mercifully softened by thick cushions) or generous oaken balconies up above and around, to face a high stage dominated by ecclesiastical artefacts, and an impressive organ of cathedral proportions. But I hadn't seen George in several weeks and was worried at what the Half-Dozen, Jacqui Dankworth and I might find. According to phonecalls George Melly was now making no sense at all. On the journey down I received texts and calls from both his friend and regular helper Michael Woods and Chris, suggesting that things might indeed be bad as George was now in very poor shape. I called Jacqui Dankworth, who was joining us on the show as usual, and suggested she bring extra music in case Chris, George's driver for the occasion, was forced to turn back. We ran through our sound check, rehearsal and first half. And then suddenly there was George.

In a wheelchair, yes, but dressed to the nines in a tailored purple velvet jacket and grey slacks, sporting a rich grey beard which lent him enormous distinction. Helped up from his chair by friendly hands, he made his steady way to centre stage amid roars of applause. And proceeded almost faultlessly through his show; coherent and cogent announcements capped by vocal contributions in a voice marginally more shaded and husky but the more attractive for that, and even rising majestically to his feet at the conclusion of 'Cakewalkin' Babies'. At the end beautiful Jacqui joined him for a joyful duo on 'Ain't Misbehaving' and the audience, as one, stood up to acknowledge the presence of a great entertainer with an ovation that rang around the ancient hall for minutes on end.

After all was done I stayed the night in London in the empty flat kindly and regularly loaned to me by old friend, Daphne Shoolman. Leaving early for a lunchtime concert in the sunshine of Golders Hill Park in Golders Green I caught a doubledecker to the station and the driver greeted me.

'Trumpet case, eh? Musician?'

'Guilty as charged,' I said.

'Me too,' said my driver, an attractive young man with an ever-present smile and strong Liverpool accent. 'Fifteen years!'

'So why are you driving a bus?'

'Well,' said my new friend. 'You know what it's like. Hand to mouth. I've got a wife and kids. And really one gig every two weeks – maybe £60 – you know what it's like. I mean if it's the right people I'll work for nothing, like we all do. But driving a bus is easy and it's regular money! Who do you work with?'

'George Melly,' I said.

His face lit up. 'George Melly! He's gold! How old is he now?'

'Eighty years,' I said, 'and nine months.'

'Bloody marvellous,' he said. 'A total hero! And who are you?'

'My name's Digby,' I said, 'Digby Fairweather.'

His face lit up again. 'Of course! I know you! I've been following you since I was that high.' His hand lowered towards the cab floor. 'Bloody wonderful. You've lost that long hair though.'

So he did know me. 'Yes,' I said.

'It's lovely having you on the bus! And you and George make a wonderful team I bet. I can't wait to see you.'

'I hope you will too – and soon!' I said, passing my friend a CD token of affection as we reached the station.

'Take care,' he called out, waving as the bus drove off amid a fanfare of toots. A wonderful team! I thought. And in the bright sun of the Golders Green Sunday morning all the church bells seemed to be ringing at once.

Over the next few days Diana was on the phone regularly.

George, she said, had not been out of bed since his Worcester triumph. But now everything was safely in place. Yes, he could continue to work around town, indeed another job had come in for July. But from mid-June, in response to medical confirmation, out-of-town jobs would be cancelled. Jack Higgins was in busy negotiation with Paul Jones and the venues concerned, and several had already agreed to take the Half-Dozen minus its featured attraction. This of course was good news; at last my band was achieving a reputation of its own it seemed. But we would miss the man who had helped us to get there.

'It's a tragedy really,' said kindly Craig Milverton, 'isn't it?'

News from the Melly household continued to be regular and constructive. George appeared on a trailer for an ITV documentary *Suggs in Soho* to be broadcast in May and, hair uncombed, bearded and sporting his most spectacular kaftan, he was looking very old: 'Terrible,' said Jack Higgins bluntly.

But filming was powering ahead. 'We're going to film him on an away job in Newark,' said Diana one morning, 'because the company wants to show how difficult it is to get him to work. And at the Testimonial concert at the 100 Club too. And by the way, he's ranting about the last album. He wants the lawyers to quash it!'

'I'm sure he won't,' I said, 'when he hears it.' And I explained about Julian's recovery from an illness and how that had slowed things up.

'I'm just warning you,' said Diana.

'Well,' I said, 'let me tell Julian. He can get a rough mix across to George and hopefully he'll be able to hear how good it is. By the way, have we an updated prognosis on his life expectancy?'

'I'd say two months,' said Diana. But next morning she was on the phone again.

'Michael came in last night,' she said, 'and he tells me that George is sinking fast. In fact I've asked the children to come in today to see him. But if he lasts the night I presume we won't need to be at Teddington until around 8.30 tomorrow. I really don't know what's going to happen. But Jacqui Dankworth does the first half of your show, doesn't she?'

'Yes, she does, but, if things are looking that bad later, do let me know. I'd like to get in to see him too, unless it's family only of course.'

'I'll let you know,' said Diana. 'Are you in all day?'

'Yes,' I said feeling miserable. Apparently the time was getting very near now when my old friend would make for the great cocktail bar in the sky.

If so, the Landmark Centre at Teddington on 17 May looked like an appropriate point of departure. Named so it was said by the Luftwaffe (who during the First and Second World Wars used it as a bombing reference), it is a church of opulent cathedralic majesty. The Half-Dozen checked for set-up and sound and walked the five hundred yards to a handy riverside tavern.

When we got back, the centre had turned into a full Hollywood set. Walkergeorge Films had done us proud. A team of cameramen and directors surrounded the rear entrance where I could see that George Melly, upright and steady-footed, was making his royal entry. Cameras and sound equipment hovered around and over the technicolour figure recording his every word, action and reaction.

Once inside he lay on a chaise-longue to rest; a camera still trained on its subject. I knelt beside him. 'How are you?' I asked.

'Dying!' he responded with a smile. 'But I'm fine for now. Just taking a rest. What time are we on?'

'About 9.15.'

'Two short ones?' he twinkled. The old teaser was still at his work.

The church was full; our band played its heroic set and

Jacqui Dankworth, as poised as ever, sang her songs. Then it was time.

'Ladies and gentlemen,' I announced. 'For the past five years we've had the delight of touring with a man who not only is our greatest singer of the blues but a British cultural icon of the highest order. It's been our pleasure and our pride. As you know he's had hard times of late but he continues to sing and to delight us all. Please welcome George Melly.'

The cameras panned in and, speedily propelled by Mike in shiny wheelchair, George arrived at the microphone in double-quick time to a roar of applause. Any lingering doubts as to whether he would be alive or able to make the show were dispelled.

'Old rockin' chair's got me . . .'

At the end the audience stood up as one to applaud their star, and his encore – a flirtatious 'Ain't Misbehaving' with Jacqui – kept them on their feet. Afterwards he was wheeled to the back lobby and at the entrance I knelt by his chair and kissed him on the cheek.

'This,' I said, 'is the greatest man in the world!'

A day or so later I was due back on the road but found time to send a letter of report to our agent down in Bradwell-on-Sea. I knew he'd been thinking about us.

Dear Jack,

As we haven't been able to talk over the last couple of days – I've been busy at theJazz recording Bank Holiday specials as well as blowing – thought you'd like an update!

Teddington was fine. George arrived in a wheelchair and was wheeled on to the stage by Mike, his minder. But he sang well and the duet with Jacqui at the end was amazing. He had a standing ovation.

He is of course getting weaker now but preserves his energy off-stage and is still mentally quite sharp I think – we had a good conversation. It's sad to see the slow departure of such a fine old trouper but I'm sure he's doing it as he wants, and the family and friends are gathering around which is good to see. I don't think we've seen the last of him quite yet . . .

Including tonight of course! Off to Newark shortly; then down West for a couple of days to do solo gigs.

Hope you're well and as busy as usual!

As ever,

Dig.

At Newark, where we played the beautiful old Palace Theatre, there were more cameras, a full house and, yet again, a tour-de-force from George. He had been unwell on the way to the theatre but once on-stage stopped the show with Jacqui and the band. Beforehand Sally, the director of Walkergeorge Films, had called me in for an on-camera interview.

'How do you feel about people telling him he should stop?' she asked.

'That's a difficult one,' I said and meant it. 'The problem is, George is of course now very ill. And all those closest to him see all of that. But there's something about the act of performance. It can lift you. And it might be difficult for even the most highly qualified doctor to understand how that can happen. But not understanding might also hurt George for as long as he's able to sing at all. Because it takes away probably his most principal pleasure now.'

'How would you feel if he were to die on stage?' asked Sally.

'Well, to be truthful, of course we hope it won't happen. But, if it did, the band and I, we'd be at his side. Bring down the curtain. And give him a round of applause to send him off.'

But after the ringing applause at Newark, the battery of cameras and brouhaha of activity, all was quiet again. A week later Diana rang to tie up details of the Melly Testimonial Concert, rapidly approaching on 10 June.

'How's George?' I asked.

'Well,' she said, 'he's been asleep since last Saturday. He hasn't got out of bed once. Which is good really, isn't it?'

But a few days later remarkable things started to happen. Paul Jones – my hero from the roaring sixties and now Britain's principal blues authority on radio (as well as still being the star frontman of both the Manfreds and his own Blues Band) – agreed to compere and Van Morrison was, by all reports, checking his commitments. And then the phone started to ring. Musicians, fans, personal friends – all had heard about the Melly Testimonial. And the word was it was already completely sold out.

On Saturday, 2 July I found a call from Diana on my answerphone. 'We're going to have to cancel Goring next Friday,' she said briefly. This was sad news; Goring Jazz Club – in a pretty village hall which was always packed to the rafters with its eminent guests – was only a manageable drive west up the Thames from Shepherd's Bush and consequently had been kept in George's schedule until now. 'But,' said Diana, 'George has hardly been out of bed since Newark. And the nurses are in every day now.' They have brought morphine and related treatments to the house in case pain kicks in. 'And we can only hope,' she said, 'that he can make the Testimonial on Sunday. Yes, we can get him there. And of course he doesn't have to do anything – except meet the people who love him.'

Now, though, things were starting to move fast. And later that day Jack was on the phone again at full power. 'George is out of action now – for good,' he said. 'And I want you to do some work for me. Find out everybody's availability for everything. He won't be doing any more at all. So get to it!'

I got to it but found it hard to get the instant answers that Jack needed. Then Goring Jazz Club, having agreed to our appearance, summarily decided to cancel it. 'We don't want the backing group,' someone said.

I was very upset. I knew we had one of the best small bands in the country but the cancellation hurt, nevertheless. Then in the evening Diana left a long message on my answerphone full of frustration and anger over the cancellation (why hadn't people taken her advice long ago, then all the jobs would have gone by now?) and that some performers had not confirmed their appearance at the benefit.

And of course the Sunday concert was sold out; no help had been needed from anyone with the publicity. It was an ugly day, and I had to work hard to remember that approaching death turns the normal niceties of living upside down.

But I couldn't help wondering what was swirling around in the still-active brain of my old friend. Now he was lying in a specially installed hospital bed downstairs in his living-room and attended at all times by Macmillan nurses and other minders, as well as by Diana. 'But,' she said, 'he's still quite cheerful and not in any pain. He knows he's dying though. And I've no idea if he'll be there for his Testimonial.'

'We'll just have to take it by the day,' I said. She agreed.

And so Sunday, 10 June arrived: the day of George Melly's Testimonial Concert. A bright optimistic morning and 'Yes,' said Diana, George would be there. Transported by an ambulance and carried down the steps of the 100 Club on a stretcher if necessary; the first time, it occurred to me, that George (so far as I knew) had been carried on to the stage rather than off it at the night's end!

Katie, from the trust for dementia, was on the phone as I hit London at 5.30 p.m.. 'The 100 Club looks great,' she said, 'and we're heading back to the Mellys to collect George. Do you think he should come on straightaway?'

'Definitely. Good idea.'

As I reached the club the queue down Oxford Street was already forming. Paul Jones, fresh faced, charismatic and looking no older than he did back in the hit-making sixties, was at the door. 'Truly good to see you,' I said, as we shook hands.

Downstairs in the club it was already a turmoil of activity. A swarm of charity workers busily buzzed around, manning buckets, and a table of T-shirts and programmes had been set up by the door. Film cameras were everywhere catching every moment. A professional recordist was behind the sound desk to record the whole concert.

The Half-Dozen arrived and we sound checked briefly just as people began to swarm into the club, running through Paul's new selections – 'I Ain't Got Nothin' but the Blues', and an up-tempo 'All Right, OK, You Win', to which I had inserted a light-hearted *Paul Jones Medley* – '54321' and 'Pretty Flamingo' converted for twelve-bar purposes. Paul enjoyed the joke and sounded wonderful, tearing into his vocals with the vigour of a twenty-year-old, and producing ecstatic harmonica solos for good measure. Even our rehearsal (minus bass as Len Skeat was lost in Clapham) received cheers. Soon the club was over-flowing; people of all kinds – from 100 Club habitués like actor John Turner and long-time Melly colleague and co-writer Michael Pointon to Melly fans from other areas of his work – had come from home and abroad for the music and to pay their respects to a legend.

But then it was time to visit George. 'He's in the dressing room,' said Paul. 'And he really doesn't look good. There's been a decline . . .' He shook his head, looking perturbed.

In the dressing room in his wheelchair was our star. Considerably shrunken (by account he had neither eaten nor drunk for three days), he looked distinguished nonetheless; his grey beard fulsome, his dress immaculate as ever. Around him, the court of King George: Diana, son Tom, granddaughter Kezzie, Candy, John Chilton looking distressed behind his old partner's wheelchair, and Michael kneeling gently at his charge's feet. As I came in he looked up and twinkled but his voice was only a whisper.

'Two short ones?'

'Not this time!' I knelt next to Michael. 'They're all here for you! The club's packed, just like sixty years ago.' He nodded but his reply was inaudible.

Michael turned to me. 'He thinks he's still in his bedroom,' he said.

Outside George Webb's Band of Brothers had completed a storming set; the bandleader, nearing ninety, playing with the same romping enthusiasm as when he'd led his legendary Dixielanders in 1943, the band that had started it all for everybody. Then, to the stage came Kenny Ball with his Jazzmen, blowing with the same power through the joyful show that had propelled him back and back to the charts at the height of the trad boom nearly thirty years on from George. In between them, Paul Jones was a charismatic master of ceremonies, bridging an unscheduled five-minute hiatus with an unexpected but expert George Burns routine, and reading goodwill messages from a star catalogue of celebrities, among them Van Morrison, Sir Paul McCartney and the politician and jazz fan Kenneth Clarke. Between bands there was an auction heroically hosted by Alan Yentob with willing help from Paul, at which a bottle of J&B Irish whiskey encased in leather fetched several hundred pounds as did a dinner for four at a prominent London restaurant. George's famed J&B striped suit fetched less than it might have but still was sold for over one thousand pounds. A raffle, occasionally chaotic, nevertheless raised more money still.

And then it was time for us. I could see George's wheelchair on its way as the Half-Dozen took the stage.

'Ladies and gentlemen,' I said, 'sixty years ago, a young man took to this stage while Humphrey Lyttelton blew his solo, eyes closed, on "Dr Jazz" and sang a chorus. Afterwards Humph said, "If you want to sing again, just ask." He brought the house down then. And he'll do so again tonight. Ladies and gentlemen [I could hear the applause rising already], please welcome our legend, George Melly.' The audience rose to its feet.

Hoisted to the stage in his wheelchair George took the microphone from Michael's hand. His voice was veiled and much of the old power had vanished but the opening line was unmistakable nonetheless.

'Old rockin' chair's got me . . .'

Clearly it hadn't quite just yet. 'Cakewalkin' Babies' followed and then a moment's silent absence as George stared vacantly into space. Michael, once again at his charge's feet, whispered, 'That's enough.'

But I was closer to my star's ear and tried for one more last long shot. 'George! "Thinkin' Blues"!'

The Half-Dozen struck up and, in little more than a hoarse whisper, he sang his last song. His audience rose to its feet again as he was carried from the stage to his dressing room and the applause refused to end. As Paul Jones bounded to the stage the joint was jumping once again to the last breathless bars.

'This has been a great night in musical history,' someone said afterwards. 'My hands were burning with clapping,' another member of the audience told me.

Mindful of my optimist's tendency to maximise the effects of a show, next morning I wanted to find out what other people thought of the concert. Had they come for a good time? To see the last musical efforts of a dying man? Or most likely, it seemed to me, to pay their respects to a legend? I telephoned Sally

George, whose unfailing sunny smile, warm affectionate nature and infectious love of life had turned us into instant friends. Sally's previous documentary, about a group of old people called *Young @ Heart*, who had defiantly toured America singing rock'n'roll music, had won two Golden Rose awards at Switzerland's Rose d'Or festival 2007.

'How was it?' I asked.

'Wonderful,' she said, 'and very moving too. Though sad of course. His son Tom was distraught. He said, "My dad thinks he's just come from a pantomime! He's not my dad any more." I know the feeling well – my father was just the same at the end. And I know that Katie, whose film it is, has been very moved and disturbed too sometimes by what she's seen. But it was just such an honour to have him there; a great man and so brave! Staring the Reaper in the face is not easy.'

'Moving' seemed to be the key word. Later in the day, two old friends rang. The first of them was double bassist Pete Corrigan. 'I had a little microphone there,' he said, 'talking to people for my radio show. And many people said the same thing: that seeing how the jazz fraternity united to celebrate a great life was deeply affecting.' But it was the secretary of the Jazz Development Trust, Sebastian Scotney, who put it most cogently. 'It was the perfect, focused moment to remember George. And everyone needed an opportunity to say goodbye. That's what the evening gave them, and you can't place a value on such a privilege.'

The testimonial concert seemed certain now to be George Melly's last triumphant bow. From now on his minders, the Macmillan nurses (visiting most days) and his family would be the ones to take care of that oh-so-astute perceptive mind as George's body gradually wound down its mechanism. We had, it seemed, all but said goodbye.

'Will you see him again?' Sally George asked.

'I honestly don't know. Work is so busy at the moment, with the book, with his last album. But I have asked Diana to let me know if things take a turn for the worse. Because I do want to be there to say a last goodbye.'

But it wasn't to be. On Monday, 2 July, Julian and I finished mixing George's last album and, next day, I wrote a two hour tribute show to the old King. I was to record it for theJazz and then, I thought, it would be easy to go and place the finished master in his hands at Shepherd's Bush. But on Thursday morning, July 5th at 8.10 a.m., the phone rang.

'Carmen Callil here', said a strong resilient voice. 'Di wanted me to tell you that George passed away last night. The nurses woke her at 2.30 and she was with him at 2.37 when he died. All is well and he died in happy circumstances'.

The old King was gone and at rest.

So, I thought – he's left us. But what he's left behind for us can never go away. No artist can leave more than that. And wherever he is – perhaps sharing a large whiskey with Mick Mulligan somewhere on their own private licensed cloud – I hope my old friend knows that.